Learning To Let Go:
When The Apology Is Not There

Author: Leslie M. Cue

Learning To Let Go: When The Apology Is Not There

by Author Leslie M. Cue

Printed in the United States of America

ISBN: Paperback-979-8-9942347-0-9

Ebook-979-8-9942347-1-6

Published by Lmcuepublishing

Author Website: https://www.lmcuepublishing.com

Cover By KingofDesigner

Editor: WriteRight

Table of Contents

Introduction

From early childhood to our golden years, humans consistently face life's challenges and successes. We encounter situations where people may not always do what's right or even do right by us. We must determine how we let uncomfortable situations effect our lives and livelihood. But what happens when you encounter individuals who have wronged you, and an apology or acknowledgment of the wrong never happens? Do we let the slights keep us from moving forward and harbor resentment and hate in our hearts or do we choose to forgive and move on?

This book, a reflection of my life and experiences, will explore situations many of us have faced and how we can decide to move forward. While we can express our emotions and disappointments, we should not allow those emotions to take control over our lives or livelihood, leaving us stunted and numb. Unless we confront what happened, determine how to approach the situation and move on, we can miss out on the life that was ordained for us. We must learn to just *let go*.

Chapter 1: My Reason For Not Staying Silent.

I f you get the pleasure of living long enough, you will have trials and tribulations. How you handle these situations will determine if you just live or live more abundantly. I choose to have an abundant life, but I had to learn how to release and let go of the things I've experienced. Was it easy? Not really. Did I have to do the hard work? Yes. And this book is the result of experiences I have had firsthand. I had to realize that if I wanted to free myself of the hurt and pain, I had to let go of some things that simply were not in my control. I had to decide that I wanted to live life fully. Oftentimes, we get caught up in what has happened to us or opportunities we missed, but we can't let those things keep us from growing and evolving.

For me, the things that really kept me from being open and experiencing new things were my lack of trust in others and the realization that I was waiting for something that was not going to happen. They weren't going to acknowledge their wrongdoing or apologize. They went on living life as if nothing had happened. And to make matters worse, the things that I allowed to bind and hinder me, resulted in my not being my best self. I often found myself withdrawn or suspicious of others. I didn't let myself enjoy the moment or I overthought it. But as different situations happened, I realized that I had to heal before I could truly be happy with myself.

Once that happened, I could be open to new experiences and enjoy a better quality of life.

My initial experience with letting go was releasing my childhood trauma. My story is one that I'm sure many others can relate to. I was raised in the South, to be exact, in a small town called Cheraw, South Carolina. My maternal grandmother, Mary Louise, raised me and gave me what she could with the limited resources she had. To keep it simple, I was, we were, poor, and I knew it. We didn't own anything but the clothes on our backs and whatever else was given to us. Every place we stayed was rented, and the properties were never in the best condition.

I was the child who grew up on food stamps and wore hand-me-downs. My exposure to life's better things came from members of my community who didn't see it as robbery to help from time to time. I think I was maybe in the sixth or seventh grade before I can remember my grandmother working a full-time job. Before, she did odd jobs like cleaning people's houses and taking care of their children. She did the best she could with only a sixth-grade education. She never learned how to drive, and if we wanted to go anywhere in town, we had to walk or depend on family members and people in our neighborhood for rides. My small town did not have a public transit system, so if you were without your own transportation, you missed out on opportunities.

Despite our physical situation, my grandmother was a soft-spoken woman who poured what she could into me. She made sure that I attended school. She allowed me to participate in activities that helped me develop and gain different experiences. And most importantly, she made sure that my basic needs, such as food and shelter, were supplied. She was really my everything, and I knew that she cared for me and her family.

But my childhood trauma doesn't come from growing up poor. Being poor was not unusual during these times. My trauma comes from knowing that I had parents who chose not to pour into or acknowledge me. My mother, for example, is still alive and well, thank God, stayed in the home with me, but she acted as if I were a stranger. There was no motherly love for me, her firstborn. She never attempted to talk to me. It was like I wasn't her child. I thought it was strange that my biological mother could be in the same home as me but not attempt to have a relationship with me. As I got older, I could see how other parents interacted with their children, which made my situation worse. And because I wasn't involved in any school or athletics activities, I was at home a lot, where she treated me as if I were invisible.

She never acknowledged my birthdays, she held no conversations with me, and when Christmas came around, I never expected much because I never received much. I have a younger sibling who was in the same household, and my mother always made sure to get him what she couldn't afford. One Christmas, I remember getting a game of chess and checkers and two pairs of corduroy pants. My brother got a four-wheeler, bike and a bunch of outfits. When I questioned why he was receiving so much while I received so little, the response was, "Well, he is a guy and it's different for him." What the h-e double hockey sticks was that all about? I knew that couldn't be the answer. The disparity had to be with the fact that my mom had a relationship with his unemployed father, who basically stayed with us off and on.

As a result, she went out of her way to provide things for my brother because she was involved with his father, even though my brother didn't really have a relationship with his dad. The difference was always there, and it was hurtful to see. I was just expected to do without because I was a female. Females are often told to be strong and just make things work, while the male children are cuddled and spoiled. When both should be taught to be self-sufficient and to do their share. But more than that, all children need love and acceptance from their parents.

While my mother was in the house and I could see her, my relationship with my father was nonexistent. There was never a discussion about him and his absence. I think I was around 12 before I even knew who my father was. It was like a scene from a movie. I was at home with my grandmother, and she got a call from my biological mother, who was at work. I don't know what the two of them talked about, but when the conversation ended, my grandmother looked at me and said that my brother was coming to see me. I had no idea how to respond because up until that point, I didn't know anything about another brother. The only brother I knew lived in the household with me. Apparently, it was an older brother, and we shared the same father.

I don't even remember the details of what happened when he came to the house, but I remember meeting him and what happened afterward. James, my newly found brother's name, comes to the house and speaks to my grandmother, Mary Louise. He comes inside the house and introduces himself as my brother and tells me that he was always told that he had another sister who stayed in Cheraw. He promised himself that when he got old enough, he would find me. I think he was about 18 or 19, and I was impressed that he wanted to find me.

Most people would not have tried since they already had established family dynamics. He goes on tell me that not only was it him but that I had two sisters as well. My biological dad was married, and he had three children with his wife. I couldn't believe it, but I was eager to get to know them and my father's side of the family. At the time, my brother was in the military and when he would come home, with permission from my grandmother, he would get me and take me to my other relatives" homes. This is when I met my paternal grandmother, Anniebelle. While I didn't know them, I was excited that James had introduced me to her and my aunts and was thankful that I had the opportunity to get to know them.

One weekend, when James picked me up, an older gentleman was sitting in the back seat of the car. I had no idea who he was and had never seen him a day in my life. And neither he nor James said who he was. By then, James was out of the military and was living in an apartment with his wife and kids. When we reached his apartment, we went in. I spoke to his wife, and as it was late, I got ready for bed. I was probably about 15 or 16; I can't remember my exact age. Anyway, James knocked on my door and asked if he could come in. I was like sure, maybe he forgot to tell me something or maybe I had left something in the car. What happened next was a memory I can't erase.

My brother comes into the room and asks me, "Do you know the man who was in the back seat with you?" I told him, "No, I never laid eyes on this man before." He then begins to tell me that the man is my father. Surely, this can't be my biological father; he didn't utter two words to me. But he was, in fact, my biological father. I told my brother that I didn't know because there was never any contact with him, whether it was phone calls or physical visits. Nothing. James assured me he was my father and that he'd be staying with my grandmother for a while. I later learned that my biological father, Roy, was away, God knows where, just away, and that he had returned home. I later learned that he left his wife and three kids, maybe when James was 12, and just returned like nothing happened.

The irony of all of this is that my biological grandmother and family only lived maybe 25 minutes away from me this whole time. But before James found me, no one had ever tried to see or reach out to me. I don't blame them, but the thought that they were so close all these years was crazy. I mean, when I look at the situation as an adult, I can see how it can be easy only to be responsible for your own household. Oftentimes, money, time and lack of resources prevent us from helping others, even if we are aware of what the situation is. Now, that does not mean, that out of 12 years that someone from my father's family could have at least tried to visit me. Especially, when several people had vehicles, and we lived so close. My father's mother, never drove a day in her life, therefore I can't necessarily blame her for anything. However, she knew about me, and it just made me wonder if I was ever on anyone's mind. I am thankful that there was at least a conversation about me, because my brother was able to search for me and get to know me.

Throughout the years, I made efforts to get to know my father's side of the family and some of the family members and I have become close. The issue, however, just like with my biological mother, is that my father never tried to get to know me or even explain why he never wanted to be in my life. To make matters worse, he was an alcoholic, and he never tried to talk to me unless he was drunk. Other than that, he, like my mom, acted as if I didn't exist. Whenever I'd go to family functions, I was always asked, "Who are you?" Now, don't get me wrong, Black people always ask who you are, particularly at family reunions and funerals.

But after a while, that question gets old. One time, when a cousin was having a conversation with my biological father in front of me, and he said to him, "I didn't know you had another child," and his response was, "Some things you keep a secret." Who in the hell makes a statement like that in front of their child? What was his problem, and why would you say that directly in front of me?

I will never know the state of my biological parents' relationship and how I was conceived, but what I do know is that there was no desire from either of them to have a relationship with me. Anyone can see how painful it is for a child to know that your parents just don't want you. I often asked my grandmother, Mary Louise, if something had happened to my mother to see if there might be a reason her reaction to me was not the same as with my brother, and my grandmother would avoid the question. My biological mother would do the same thing, and would just say, "The past is the past." I never received anything to fill the void and or get an explanation for their behavior.

My biological father and some of his family members felt that even though he abandoned his family and children, it was okay because plenty of people don't have intact families. To make matters worse, at the end of my biological father's life, he was diagnosed with lung and throat cancer. The same family members commented to other family members that I should have been there for my father at the end and helped take care of him. One of them even had the nerve to say, "I should be ashamed of myself for not stepping in and taking care of my father." Luckily, I had a very close family member who is like a brother to me to put him in his place. As a matter of fact, he told that family member that he needed to play the whole tape, and that my biological father hadn't been there for me, and everyone seemed okay with that.

Why was it different now? He abandoned me, but I'm expected to care for him when he's old and sick. People want children to honor their parents, but they couldn't care less if the parents don't honor the children. He suffered his last days, and cancer killed him. I did go to his funeral service and opted to sit on the opposite side of the family. This caused tension as some family members were upset that I didn't step in to take care of my biological father. Out of respect, I went to the service, but I didn't and couldn't cry, because I did not have a relationship with this person. At his end, he could not tell me anything about my life, and I couldn't tell him anything about his.

An uncle's ex-wife sat behind me in the church. While the service was underway, I overheard this so-called woman of God tell the person sitting next to her that she didn't know why I wasn't sitting with the family. "Her dad loved her," she said. "She should be ashamed." Now, who the hell are you talking to at somebody's funeral, and let's not play these games. My biological father was not a good man. He abandoned his family, and at the end he had nothing to show for it. When people use the word love, I don't think they really know what it means. Loving someone means that you are going to honor them, take care of them, provide for them, pray for them and, guess what, be there for them! He lived a hard life and ran away from his responsibilities. That man didn't love me, and his actions proved that. STOP TRYING TO MAKE THESE PEOPLE SAINTS BECAUSE THEY ARE DEAD!

All my life I wanted to feel a part of a family. When you don't grow up in a family, you can't envision what it means and thus recreate it later. The dynamics are not there, no matter how you try to assimilate into the family. It is kind of like you are always the outside kid, constantly reminded of it. I have no idea what happened with my paternal parents and what caused our relationship to be null and void. I would often go through what if this happened or maybe this is why it all happened to try and justify their actions. More specifically, I noticed when my biological father died that the age difference, between he and my mother was a whooping 15 years.

My mom had me at 18, according to my birth certificate, and my father was 33 years old and married with kids. How exactly did they get involved, and what were the dynamics of that relationship?? I had the pleasure of knowing my stepmother, Betty and she would often tell me that she never blamed my mother for the relationship because my mother was so young. My mother grew up on a farm and my grandmother, Mary Louise, often said my mom would go missing. Was this a situation where she was being taken advantage of? I will never know, but what I do know is that whatever happened caused her not to want a relationship with me.

I believe this was a situation where she was sweet-talked by an older man who took advantage of her naiveness. And her being pregnant probably resulted in her enduring some backlash from the community and family. Our community was small, and everyone knew everybody, and word travels. To be that young and for everyone to know you are carrying a married man's child must have been tough. I assume seeing me was a reminder of whatever happened. I can have empathy for her, but at the same time be remorseful that both of my parents sucked at parenting me. I wish I could say something different, but it's how I feel, and it's the reality of the situation. While I have grown from this, I am still emotional. My biological mother is alive, and while we don't have the best relationship, we are cordial, and I do visit and spend time with her. It's just not a bubbly motherly relationship because my mother figure, my grandmother, Mary Louise, has died. I had to forgive my parents to move forward. I don't like carrying around anger, and I don't want to display it to my own child. I know what I needed as a child, and I wanted to be a better parent for my daughter. Every chance I get, I tell her and show her how much I love and support her.

While dealing with the issues with my biological father, I realized that no matter what he did, some family members were going to support him and invalidate my feelings. We are taught to take care of our family. But if your family is wrong, it's probably best to stay silent instead of trying to support or make excuses for their wrongdoing. I have a right to talk about my feelings, and they have the right not to agree with me, but let's not paint a picture of someone they are not. Family or not, if you are not a good person, you are not a good person. If you choose to disrespect me or try to discredit me because I am expressing my feelings and my hurt, then you don't need to be in my life. I can't keep talking to you about the same thing over and over. At some point, we will agree just to disagree and let it go.

By now, you get the gist of my childhood trauma. But what does that have to do with me as an adult? As I mentioned before, my grandmother, Mary Louise, took on the responsibility of caring for me. I am grateful that I was not given up for adoption, and that I did at least have one surrogate parental figure in my life. My grandmother made sure that I graduated from high school, and afterward, she would send me money when she could while I was in college. I always felt indebted to her because she took on the role of a parent. Once I got my first real job, she would often reach out to me for money, and I would send it to her with no problem. After all, she did raise me with what little she had. Even though by this time, I was a single parent working full-time with a 2-year-old. My own bills were adding up, and by the time I paid rent, utilities, car insurance, daycare, cell phone, cable, student loan, internet, food, clothing and copayments for doctor visits, I was left financially strapped. I really didn't have extra money to do much, and my entertainment was often a movie rental from Blockbuster and later Redbox. If I went out to eat, it was only occasionally, and my meal cost less than $20. Despite that, I still made every effort to send my grandmother money whenever she needed it. Oftentimes, that was every two weeks. It was like as soon as I got paid, she was calling and asking for money. By now, she was much older and not working. Her main source of income was Social Security SSI, and I understood being on a tight budget because I was on one myself, but I was giving away money I really didn't have. What could I say, I mean, I didn't want to appear ungrateful, because she did raise me, but at the time, I just didn't have it like that. To make matters worse, I worked in customer service right after college, and while the money was decent, the job was stressful. I tried my best by showing my grandmother that I appreciated and cared for her by going to visit her often, calling to check on here and always making sure that I got her nice gifts for Mother's Day, her birthday and, of course, Christmas. I sometimes laugh at myself now because her favorite store was Hamrick's. And where do I shop now, that's right, Hamrick's.

Chapter 2: It's Okay To Say No

After all I went through during my childhood, being an adult brought on new traumas. My stress now was my job, and with being a new mom, trying to make sure I was providing for my child, who was primarily my priority. My daughter was always sick between the ages of 2 to 6. She kept ear and sinus infections, and if she had both at the same time, that meant I had to take a vacation day(s) to take care of her. Nothing over the counter ever worked, and we stayed at the pediatrician. I used my vacation days for her sick days and could never really save much when she was younger. Now, when you factor that in, on top of my normal expenses, imagine trying to take care of someone else's household. Like I said before, I felt obligated to help my grandmother, but it pushed me over the edge and stressed me out. Sometimes I would even overdraft my account trying to send money home.

I can remember talking to my aunt Ann and asking her why Grandma always needed money, and she laughed at me. I was like, "Why are you laughing?" Her response was, because she doesn't. She is asking you for money to help your mom with her bills." She was like, "Your mom isn't going to ask, since the two of you don't have a relationship; she gets your grandma to ask." Here I was stressing myself out to help who, I thought, needed help, only to find out I was being used. I'm not saying I wouldn't help my mother, but I shouldn't have been lied to. Knowing all that, I still sent the money because I didn't know how to tell my grandmother "No."

As time went on, my job became more stressful. Every day, I started looking for something new. Although I disliked the job, it was my source of income until I could find something better. One day, I was having one of the worst phone calls, or at least it appeared that way. A business associate from a doctor's office called to verify benefits. Normally, those calls are a breeze, but this one struck a nerve. The representative would give me the patient's information, and I would verify the benefits. Initially, she wanted me to check for one patient.

When that was complete, she had a second patient. This continued for the third and fourth patients. For whatever reason, I just lost it. I told her we had a dedicated line for multiple patients, and then I transferred her. Thirty minutes later, my supervisor, Mary, came to my desk and said she needed to talk to me. I logged off, and went to her office, and took my purse with me.

I had no idea what was going to happen, but I was going to be prepared. I didn't keep pictures or anything on my desk. Mary was sweet and asked me about the call. I told her that the business associate kept saying one more even though she had several, and that I had transferred her to the multiple line.

She continued to say that the representative said that I had an attitude and wasn't being professional. To be honest, I probably did and really couldn't make an excuse for it. Mary then asked, "Is everything okay? You don't seem yourself." And it was at this point that the stress of everything just crashed down on me. I was like, "No, I'm not okay, and I am just sick and tired of everything." Out of nowhere, I started crying, and I couldn't control it.

At some point, I think I slammed my hands on the desk. It felt like an out-of-body experience. Poor Mary probably didn't know how to respond, but what she did next changed my life. Mary said, "You have been with the company for a while, and we have an employee assistance program where you can talk to someone." She gave me their phone number and told me to investigate taking a mental health leave. She explained the process and told me to take vacation time for the rest of the day. She informed me that she taken leave while she was dealing with personal matters and that it might benefit me to talk to someone about how I was feeling. I went home, sat on my living room chair, and stared at the wall.

I had never opened up to anyone other than my close friends about my feelings, and I didn't know how I would feel talking to a stranger about such personal matters. But I also needed someone to help me understand what I was going through and how to get out of this funk. I didn't know how to let go.

Whatever was going on with me, affected my mood and I was feeling defeated, tired and hopeless. This uneasiness was affecting both my personal and professional life. I decided to call my employee assistance program line and spoke to a representative who was very empathetic. She asked me if I was a threat to myself or others, and I advised her no, but that I was just feeling hopeless and depressed. She had me describe what was going on, and I let her know that I was feeling the pressure of trying to be there for myself, my child and my family, and that emotionally and financially, I could no longer do it.

In addition, my job was very stressful and that it was becoming harder to just show up. She asked me if I would be okay with speaking with someone, and I told her that, at this point, I was willing to do whatever it took to get better. She asked was there a preference and I advised her no, but I did want to speak with someone who had a background in theology/religion but was also a trained counselor. She referred me to a counselor, and I was able to get an appointment the following week. In the meantime, I was placed on medical leave, and my supervisor advised me to complete my paperwork to ensure I would be paid while I was out. I felt some relief just being out of work, but I knew that something had to give, and I didn't know where to start.

My appointment eventually came, and I went as scheduled. I checked myself in with the receptionist and waited in the lobby. After about 10 minutes of waiting, my counselor came to the lobby and asked me to come back for our session. I followed him to the patient room and sat down in a very comfortable chair. My counselor immediately made me feel comfortable by formally introducing himself and providing his credentials. He informed me that he was a retired pastor with 20 years of experience and a licensed professional counselor. Therefore, his experience was extensive as he counseled individuals from different walks of life and could provide different perspectives. This was good to hear because my faith is important to me. But I knew that I needed God *and* a counselor.

I think our visit started out normally as he asked me what led me to counseling. Before I knew it, the tears started, and I just let everything out. Not only was my stress related to just always feeling like I never had enough financially, but I felt so guilty that I couldn't give to my grandmother. I loved this woman, and I know she made a sacrifice to take care of me. I guess I just felt that being in my early 20s, my life would be set up a little better, and that I should be doing more for myself. This was the first on many visits and it felt so refreshing to just go to each visit. I looked forward to my visits every week and just getting everything out.

On one visit, my counselor asked me about my reasons for taking on the financial responsibility of providing for my grandmother. I mean, I was the granddaughter, but the reality was that she had four adult children. I never thought of it like that, but I explained to him that I wanted to take care of her because she took care of me. The next question threw me off a little, but it was something that I never thought of. He asked me did she make the decision to take care of me or was she forced to take care of me? I sat for a couple of minutes because I really had to think about this question. My grandmother never made me feel like she was forced to take care of me; it was just something she did. My counselor then stated that we could conclude she decided to be your parent.

I agreed with that conclusion. He then asked me as a parent myself would I obligate my daughter to financially take care of me for the rest of my life. I think my brain cells were jumping all over the place because I was trying to understand the magnitude of the question he was asking. I started just blurting out my answers. No and yes were my answers. I did expect my daughter to one day help take care of me if I were unable to take care of myself physically and, I guess, financially.

However, I was going to do my best to prepare for my future and take care of myself. My goal would be to help her with her family and possibly my grandchildren. I don't see myself just asking my daughter for money, but I expect to spend time with her and form bonds with her future family. He asked me do I expect adults to take care of themselves? My response was "Yes." I mean, not everyone may have the same opportunities, but I do feel that, at the end of the day, we can all work hard and provide for our own needs. If people help you, whether it's family or friends, it's because they want to, and not because it is their responsibility.

What he told me next really made me put things into perspective. He advised me that, based on what I had said to him, my obligation to my grandmother stemmed from her decision to take care of me in the absence of my parents. When you choose to become someone's parent, you take all the responsibility that comes along with it. He said Leslie, you didn't ask her to take on this responsibility of caring for you. She chose this responsibility, and therefore, it should not be something anyone is keeping over your head. By her constantly expecting you to take care of her household, she is saying to you that you owe her.

That's not what parents do to their children. Children don't owe their parents for being born because they didn't ask to be born. Even though most families will take on the responsibility of caring for another family member's child(ren), there is always an option for adoption. Who is to say that your life would have been better or worse? Every adoption story is not horrible.

But what you can't do is keep putting yourself under this pressure to try to pay back a debt that shouldn't be there. In other words, the bank is now closed, and that is what you must start saying. No, is a complete sentence. If it makes you feel better, you can say, "No, I have responsibilities at home, and my household currently does not allow me to help anyone else." If you don't start using that word, you will continue to stress yourself out, and that won't be good for the child you are taking care of. How can I tell someone who made sure I was taken care of "No?" It was not something that I was sure I could do, but I also knew that I could not continue to hand out money I couldn't afford to give. I had to set some boundaries, and I knew that it was going to be quick because, like clockwork, every two weeks, I was going to get a call.

The next issue we addressed was abandonment. Based on my comments, my counselor reiterated that my bond with my grandma was built out of my commitment to her as well as my need to have someone that I could relate to and rely on. In other words, all I knew was my grandma and her actions showed me that I could count on her. The actions of my biological parents, however, showed me the opposite. Because I did not want to lose the connection I had with my grandma, I continued to put myself in danger financially. It was basically like I didn't' want to lose the one person I knew had my back.

I never really thought about it this way, but it made perfect sense. My counselor also pointed out that when people genuinely care for you, they would respect your boundaries, and if your relationship ended because you set boundaries, then let's just say you really didn't have a relationship. It would be hard at first but saying no was something that I had to stay firm on, especially if I wanted to make some changes in my life. This was a lesson I had to learn. Not just for my grandmother, but in all circumstances.

As expected, my grandma called, and we went through the formalities of her asking me how everything was going with me and my daughter. I responded things were going okay and that I had taken some time off work because I was little stressed, and I needed to do some self-care. I asked how she was doing and if anything, new was going on in our town? She responded that she was okay, and the next question was, "Well, I was wondering if you could send me $100 dollars?" I need to pay a bill, she added.

Now, if it was really her bill or not, I wasn't sure, but I knew that the time had come to say, "No." To some people, $100 is pocket change, but for me, it was a lot. At the time, I was only making like $30,000 a year, and if you counted all my monthly bills, I might be left with only $200 to $300 of extra money each month. Most of my money each month went towards bills and other expenses. Also, I remembered what my auntie said about her asking for my mother, not her.

Not that I had a problem helping my biological mom, but I just have memories of her never wanting to help me. I could recall several instances where she refused to help me. During my sophomore year of college, I really needed a car. I didn't know the importance of credit, didn't have a credit score, and I was trying to get reliable transportation to get back and forth from school and to get a job off campus, making more money. Several of my friends had cars, but they went home on the weekends to work, and their parents helped them buy one.

I think I was being naïve because I thought maybe my biological mom would want to co-sign for me a car since she had good credit, to my knowledge. So, I got up the courage and called home and asked her. Well, when I called home, I told her my dilemma and asked her if she would help. I mean, she didn't help me with anything else; of course, she would want to help me. I was working, keeping my grades up, and had even received several scholarships. Do you know she told me no and didn't even offer to help with anything. Now, that angered me because soon after I found out that she co-signed for her boyfriend a car but wouldn't do it for her child.

On another occasion, I was a college senior. I worked a work-study job to help with my tuition during the week and on the weekend, I was a resident assistant for my dormitory. Money was tight, but I was able to budget what I had and make do. Well, my senior year was different, and I had extra fees of paying for my cap and gown and my senior fees. I also remember taking senior graduation pictures and getting outfits for that and paying a photographer. I called my grandma at home and told her about my extra fees and asked for some assistance.

This was my last year of college, and I needed help. She told me she really did not have it, but she would ask my biological mom. I will never forget what happened next. I was walking through Massachusetts Hall at my college, which happened to be where the registrar's office was located, when I suddenly heard someone calling out my full government name.

I turned around, and it was the registrar, telling me that she had to tell me what just happened. I started freaking out because is this going to affect my graduation? She was like, "Girl, your mother just called here asking if there really was such a thing as senior dues because she didn't know if I was telling the truth." I was so embarrassed and pissed at the same time. My biological mom had no idea what was going on with my life or what school fees were because she was never involved with my life. I didn't even know how to respond to her, and luckily, she just laughed it off. I kept thinking the whole office was probably laughing at me.

My grandma and my biological mother's relationship, in my opinion, was built on co-dependency. My biological mom was still in the same household with my grandma, while all her other children left as soon as they were 18 and out of high school. It was like my biological mom was a failure to launch story. I really couldn't explain it, but it was like one couldn't do anything without the other. My whole childhood and adulthood, my biological mom worked a full-time job but was never independent.

The words that came out of my mouth next must have been from God. I told my grandmother I didn't have it, and as a matter of fact, I probably wouldn't have it soon because I needed to focus on taking care of myself and my household. There was silence for a minute, and then she asked could I send her maybe $75 instead. Once again, I responded "No." I don't think she was expecting no as an answer, but she said "Okay," and that she would talk to me later.

She didn't seem upset, and I felt relieved. I was worried because I kept thinking, what if she really needed the money and something was in jeopardy of getting cut off, but then I was like, she would have said that. I went back to counseling for my next visit, and I was happy to report to my counselor that I was able to say no to my grandma. He asked me how that made me feel? And my response was, "I'm not sure how that made me feel, but I knew it was necessary."

I wish I could say that it was the last time I had to enforce saying no, but it wasn't. Several times after that, she would still call and ask, and after maybe three or four times, she got the picture. I continued to do for her as I could and made sure that I called and physically went to see her. I gifted her things when I could and let her know she was important to me. Our relationship remained strong until the day she went to be with the Lord.

I didn't know it then, but learning to say no was also a step toward me moving beyond my childhood trauma. I realized my past was indeed my past and that I was responsible for the actions I took from then on. I'd finally learned how to let go of my childhood traumas and fears of being abandoned. Or so I thought.

Chapter 3: I Lost My Best Friends

Once we move beyond family hurt, many of us have faced friend trauma. It's natural to form bonds with people who we grow up with or who we meet through our career paths or school. I was lucky enough to meet two people who had an impact on my life, but unfortunately, our friendship ended because of disagreements. Ironically, both of my best friends have the same first name, and I viewed them as my sisters. I grew up with my first best friend. I'm going to call her Susie 1. We went to middle and high school together, and she was my child's godmother and was one of my closest friends. We went to the same schools, and we had the same classes together. We talked on the phone and hung out, and after high school, we both went our separate ways, but our friendship continued once we moved to the same town.

Just like any other friend, we shared the most intimate parts of our life, and we shared our dreams and aspirations. In time, our friendship just grew. When I became pregnant at 23, she was the first person I told. My cycle was late, and I thought maybe it was because I was stressed out. I went to her apartment and told her I just wasn't feeling right. She happened to have some pregnancy test, and I took two pregnancy tests. Waiting for those five minutes to get the results seemed like forever, but she just encouraged me and talked about how she wanted to be a mom. She was good with children and worked at a local daycare center. She asked me how I would feel if the results came back positive, and I told her scared. At the time, I wasn't married, and I had always said that if I had a child, I would be because I did not want to be a single parent. In addition, being a parent is just nerve-wracking, and in today's world, there is so much you must shield them from.

Well, the results were in, and both came back positive. I was in such denial that we went to the store and got two more tests. Of course, those came back positive as well. I finally made a doctor's appointment, and the doctor confirmed that I was six weeks pregnant. I cried in the doctor's office because of the uncertainty of what was going to happen next, and my doctor reminded me that it was a miracle to even get pregnant.

I called my friend and told her the news and she reminded me that despite it not being planned that I was going to be a good mom, and she would be there for me. Fast forward nine months, and I gave birth to a beautiful seven-pound and nine-ounce baby girl. I asked Susie 1 to be the godmother, and she graciously agreed. She was there for her dedication to God and was very active in her life. Our friendship continued to grow, and my daughter adored her. So, you might be saying to yourself, "What happened?". Well, like anything else, a small misunderstanding can end any relationship. But unknowingly, I was processing what happened as abandonment.

I'll never forget the day. I was at work, and Susie 1 kept texting me to call her because it was an emergency. I stepped away from my desk and gave her a call. I had no idea what happened and was praying everything was okay. She answered my call and told me that she got into an argument with her boyfriend, and that things had gotten heated. This all happened the night before, and he had left their home. When she got up the next morning to go to work, her car wouldn't start. She went to look under the hood, and her engine was sitting underneath her car. It was like someone had intentionally cut the wires. She couldn't prove it was her boyfriend, and she was without a car. She asked if she could get my car to run some errands and to see if she could get someone to repair her car. I agreed, and shortly after that, she arrived with her cousin to get my car. I was in shock when I saw her face and the bruise; apparently, the argument turned physical. I had been around her boyfriend plenty of times, and she had been with him for several years.

There was never a sign or mention that he was abusive, and it concerned me. She assured me that he was no longer there and that things just got out of hand. Either way, she needed to get her car back on the road because it was all she had to get to work. She assured me she was physically okay, but, of course, emotionally it was a lot to deal with.

For the next couple of days, we carpooled, and she was finally able to find a mechanic to repair her car. But, she didn't have all the money to pay the repair bill, and now that her boyfriend was gone, she was paying the bills by herself. She asked if she could borrow $500 to assist with making the car repairs. At the time I had the money, and I told her, "Yes, of course you can." She had never asked me for anything before, and she was a good friend and Godmother to my daughter. On several occasions, she would style my daughter's hair for me because that was one thing I was not good at. I tried my best, but I could never seem to get her parts straight, and my braiding technique was not the best.

In addition, she would keep my daughter for me while I ran errands or just to give me a break. While $500 is a lot of money, I was confident that she would pay me back. We did not put a certain date that she had to pay me back, but instead I asked her to just make payments until she paid me off. I didn't immediately ask for the money back because I know that when you are trying to get back on track, it may take a while.

Weeks and months went by, and we were keeping in contact, and she would pick my daughter up from time to time. One day she kept my daughter for me because the in-home daycare closed for the day unexpectedly. When I went to pick my daughter up, I noticed that she kept going back to the spare bedroom. I didn't say anything to my friend, but obviously someone was there.

When I left and got my daughter in her car seat to take her home, I asked her how her day was and what she did with her godmother." My daughter responded that she played with Uncle Joseph and God Mommy. It was then that I knew she had taken back her ex-boyfriend. Relationships are complicated, but I couldn't figure out why she allowed him back; however, I wasn't going to question her. As time went on, she became more open with their relationship and did not try to hide it from anyone.

She, at this point, still did not make any attempts to start paying me back. I don't like bringing up money, but after about 90 days, things seemed back to normal for her, so I asked her to start making payments to me to repay the $500 she borrowed. She responded that she would, but I started noticing that our phone calls were becoming less frequent and, as a matter of fact, she often wouldn't answer my call. This concerned me because I hadn't done anything to her that would cause her to ignore my calls.

I kept thinking that maybe something else happened that I didn't know about. One day, I drove by her apartment and decided to pop up when I knew she would be home. When I pulled up, both her and her boyfriend's cars were out front. I got out and knocked on the door. I could hear the television playing inside, but nobody answered. After about three knocks, I left. But I immediately called her on her cell phone and left a message. She never called me back, and it was like she just disappeared off the face of the earth, at least to me.

Well, this is where things really started going left. Social media has become our way of staying in touch with family and friends. And while it's a good thing, it can also be a bad thing. One day, I happened to be strolling through my timeline, and pictures of her at a casino in New Orleans popped up. She was traveling with her family and friends, and it looked like they were having a great time. At this point, getting my money back became more about principle than anything else. You knew that you owed me money, and at a vulnerable time in your life, I was there for you, and you chose not to pay me one red cent back.

What was really going on, and why would you ignore me? I picked up the phone again and called her, and to no avail, still no answer. I left another voicemail. Weeks passed by, and I felt disrespected and ignored. My daughter had a relationship with her, and I treasured our friendship. At this point, I just decided that I was just going to let it go. Our friendship was more important, and I wanted her in my life.

I made another call, but this time I left a voicemail letting her know that I was just going to forgive the debt and that our friendship was more important. I urged her to please give me a call and then ended the call. Several weeks, months and then years went by and still no word from my friend.

It was around December 2009 when a mutual friend reached out to me via Facebook Messenger, asking me if I had heard from Susie 1. I told her it had been several years since I had spoken to or seen her. There was no other message from this mutual friend.

Unexpectedly, Susie 1called and apologized for everything. She was working and staying in the next town over. Then she said she had stage four breast cancer. I had mixed emotions. While I was happy to hear from my friend, I was sad to think about the health issues she was facing. She was probably about 32 years old, and she was battling late-stage cancer. About two weeks later, Susie 1's mother contacted me to say that she was in hospice care and that there was nothing else the doctors could do. Are you kidding me? We finally make amends, and she is getting ready to leave this earth? I asked her mom if we could visit her, and she replied, "Of course." She was in a local hospice care facility in our town less than 15 minutes away. I took my daughter with me, not really knowing what to expect, but for her to see her one last time. What happened next was something I could never have imagined.

I had never visited anyone in hospice before, and for some reason, I just pictured her being herself. But instead, when I walked in the room, all I saw was this fragile woman who appeared to be less than a hundred pounds, and she had lost all her hair. She was in so much pain that she was heavily medicated. I spoke to her and gave her a hug, but at this point in her life, she was grasping for air and holding on to what was left. My daughter didn't recognize her and kept asking who she was.

After years of friendship, this is how things were going to end. No time for reconciliation or to make new memories. I'm sad to say that not even a week later she passed at the age of 32. My dear friend was gone, and there was nothing I could do about it. Who would have thought that money would change the direction of our friendship? I lost a friend, and my daughter lost a second mother figure. I am not sure how I was able to move forward, but I was able to get back to normal slowly. But that feeling of being abandoned resurfaced.

Then, I didn't seek counseling but, looking back, I should have taken advantage of grief counseling. I received some closure knowing that I'd made several attempts to contact her and to rekindle the friendship. But no matter what, I can never get the time lost back. Money changes things, situations and people. What I learned from this loss of friendship was that if you don't really have it to give, then don't give. I am not saying people shouldn't pay you back what is owed, but are you willing to lose the relationship if you don't get it back? The relationship was so much more important than the money.

The second friendship loss happened later in life (about two years ago), and this loss did result in my seeking grief counseling. Grief was the emotion I experienced because when the friendship ended, it felt like death to me. The truth of the matter, however, is that the person is still physically alive.

As I mentioned earlier, both of my previous best friends had the same name. I don't think there is anything coincidental about this, but who knows. I formed this friendship with Susie 2 while we were college freshmen. We had the same major, were in the same classes and stayed in the same dorm our freshman and sophomore years. Our bond grew even closer when we pledged the same sorority. We also had similar backgrounds, as we both came from single-mother households and vowed to live differently.

We had dreams and goals, and we consistently encouraged each other to follow them. Our bond continued to grow even after college. While we were separated by distance, we stayed in contact by phone. And let me tell you, once you got us on the phone, the conversations would last for hours. We would talk about everything under the sun, and of course, what was going on in our lives. As Susie 2 moved to several different states, our friendship continued.

I would often travel to where she was, and she would do the same. Our visits normally lasted a couple of days, but we always made sure to keep in contact. I had attended the college homecomings where she taught, and she would always let me know when it was coming up. She would say, "Les, our homecoming is coming up in October, and we are having this person and these activities. Let me know if you are coming so I can plan." My daughter and I went to several homecomings with her and her daughter and had a great time.

We literally talked to each other at least four to five times weekly for 20 years. I know, you might be asking how that is possible, but believe me, it is. When you saw her, you also saw me. It was so crazy, but people would ask about her whenever they saw me because they were so used to us being together. And she got the same questions.

Just like any other friendship, our bond continued to grow, and our children shared a bond. She was a part of our family, and I think at some point we were a part of hers. We supported each other, shared milestones, corrected each other in love and, if our behavior was out of the norm, we picked up the phone and talked about it.

We gave our opinions on relationships, career choices, location changes, our families and our children. Not at any time in our friendship that spanned over 25 years did our opinion about each other's situation(s) cause us to not talk to each other. We talked whenever and it was like we knew what each other was thinking. It was so funny, but if we saw something on social media that sparked our attention, of course, that resulted in a phone call. It would be like, "Girl, did you see that post?" and "What was that all about?" Her phone number was one I had memorized, was on speed dial and I knew it by heart.

I introduced her to my friends, and they became friends. We had a bond that I never thought would be broken in a million years. That is why I use the term grief because, as you can see, we had what I thought was a lifelong bond that was unfortunately broken beyond repair. This next set of events is difficult to discuss, but it is necessary in my journey of letting go.

The unraveling of our friendship probably started in January 2022. I use that month because that's when things started taking a turn in her life. She, just like many others, longed for companionship and a commitment before God. At that time in my life, I had that desire as well, but because I was exhausted from trying to date, I temporarily gave it up. I mean, you go through the hassle of trying to be your authentic self and be transparent, and you will still meet people who play with your emotions and time.

So, as a personal choice at that time, I chose to take a break from dating. Susie 2 let God know her desires for a husband. It was important to her, and we discussed what it would look like to have a complete family. Just like any other time, we discussed what we wanted for our futures and provided encouragement.

Fast forward, she met a gentleman and told me she was going to see where it went. He had the qualities that she wanted in a mate. She gave me his background information, like we would do for anyone we were dating. I didn't think anything about it, and as a matter of fact, she called me when they went on their first date and gave me the details of the evening. She seemed excited, and just like with anything that is new, you go out on dates and talk to each other on the phone several times. It's all a part of the dating cycle. Our phone calls started to become less, and at that point I didn't take it as anything personal because that's what happens when you date and another person is introduced to the mix.

As the months went on, it was the little things that showed me that our relationship dynamics were changing. In celebration of our silver status in our sorority, we decided to go to the region where we attended college and were initiated for our sorority conference. As always, we were roommates and spoke often about celebratory activities for this milestone. We met each other at the hotel, checked in, got dressed and headed to registration. What we've always done. We were excited and couldn't wait to meet with our other sorority sisters. For the most part, the trip was going very well. However, two incidents rubbed me the wrong way, but I didn't say anything because it was supposed to be a celebration trip.

During the conferences, we decided to check the vendors out and wander around before the next scheduled activity. Suddenly, she gets a call from the man she's dating. I guess, at this point, his official title had become boyfriend. I just figured he was calling to check in with her and nothing more. As we went from vendor to vendor looking over stuff, it was like I was no longer present. As a matter of fact, she turns around and tells me, "Oh, you can just walk ahead." I was thinking, "Are you dismissing me like I'm a child? At any rate, I continued browsing through the vendors and made a couple of purchases. I briefly saw her, and she was still on the phone with him. I just went outside the vendor area, found a seat and sat down. I noticed he called her and texted her several times a day while we were on our three-day conference, and while I understood the newness of any relationship, I just kept thinking, we only physically see each other maybe twice a year. You will see that man when you get back home. But I just made the best of the trip because we were there to celebrate. At the end of the trip, we decided to go to one of the celebrity restaurants before we headed back home.

You'd think that the conversation would be ongoing since we were leaving shortly, but instead, she was glued to her phone with her boyfriend. At certain points in my conversation, I had to repeat myself because, of course, she was talking to him. She wasn't even looking at me because her eyes were glued to her phone, as she was texting him so much. While I was happy that she was getting the attention she wanted from this relationship, I couldn't help but notice how her interaction with me had changed in a short period. Quite frankly, I thought she was being quite rude. To me, it didn't matter who she was texting, it was the point of the lack of interaction.

As time went on, there were, of course, conversations between us about their relationship. Nothing out of the norm. One time, she mentioned that he dated her through her love languages. She was getting what she wanted in a relationship, but once again, I couldn't help but notice how her demeanor toward me changed. Our telephone calls were less frequent, and when we did talk it was for shorter periods, as she was preoccupied with him. Sometimes she would cut me off mid-sentence when we would speak on the phone. I was like what is this all about. It was like we were starting to play phone tag and suddenly, I was being erased.

I remember a conversation that I believe was the ending of our years of friendship. While she was telling me about their dates, she mentioned marriage. I can't really tell you exactly what she said, but I told her I was happy she was dating and to wait and see what happens at six months. I wanted her to be happy but advised her to take her time to get to know him. I didn't think I was telling her anything negative. In my opinion, they were in the honeymoon stage of the relationship.

Normally, the first couple of months it's all glitz and glamour but as time goes on you start to see their flaws. If you make it to six months, then great, but once people really start to get comfortable with you, then you start to notice things. Their real self-shows up, and their habits are exposed. All these things are normal, and it doesn't mean the individual is a bad person, but in the beginning all the bells and whistles are being pulled out to impress you.

She appeared to be taken aback that I gave her this advice, but I wasn't sure why because she had given me the same advice previously when I was dating. It was as if she was surprised by what I said, but to me, I wasn't doing anything I wouldn't normally do. Well, at least that is what I thought based on our previous experiences.

In the coming months, I continued to see more changes in our friendship. Days turned into weeks, and it was basically like a hit or miss when we did talk. I started noticing that activities that we participated in together, were no longer being presented. By now, her world seemed to revolve around him and his friends. When I finally talked to her, I mentioned that I saw that she had gone to an activity that I normally get an invite to. She just brushed it off. The truth of the matter is that I was no longer a part of the equation. By now, you might be saying, "Leslie, you are tripping, and this is what people do when they are in relationships." But was I really tripping, that I was no longer being included?

By the time November came, I was in a state of depression. Not because I knew that our relationship was ending, but because of her reaction to me. Suddenly, she started making these Facebook posts about friendships and people waiting for your relationship to end. It came out of left field because Susie 2 didn't post negative stuff on her page. But it seemed personal, and I couldn't help but think she was posting about me. While she wasn't talking to me directly, it seemed she was sending me messages. Or at least that's how I saw it.

November is a month that I always celebrate because I celebrate several milestones in my life during this month. That year was horrible for me, and I felt like I was just drowning in sorrow. To make matters worse, the mutual friends I had introduced her to started noticing her posts and asked me what was up with her. I really didn't know what was up, but I knew these were attacks against me. I was trying to stay positive and just celebrate without thinking about her social media posts. Our mutual friend invited me out for dinner for my birthday, and I was happy to celebrate with friends. I got all dressed up and met my friend at a nice restaurant, and to my surprise, four of my other friends were there. It was the picker upper I needed. I was so thankful to see their smiling faces, and the conversation and laughs just started flowing.

On this terrific Thursday I was telling them all about my plans to head to my college homecoming on the weekend. My daughter was accompanying me, and I couldn't wait to celebrate. Then they asked me a question, that just made me ball out in tears. What is going on with you and your friend Susie 2? I can't explain it, but it was like all my pain just came out. I have no idea what was going on, but it just appeared that now that the new man was in her life, she was kicking me to the curb.

My friends were mutual friends with her, and they said they noticed that she was posting all this stuff about friendship on her page. One of my friends said she even noticed that she was making comments under everything she posted and that was not normal, because she never commented on anything she posted. It was like she was trying to go out her way, to make it known. I told her I wasn't sure about our friendship, but since she started dating this guy, she no longer needed me. Also, I felt like once I expressed to her that she needed to take her time, she took that as me attacking her and her new boyfriend. Now several of my friends are married, and they felt that the advice I gave was not malicious.

It is just the truth of the matter. We all give each other advice about relationships, and that doesn't mean you are against anybody." I told them that was how she is obviously viewing it, and that we really didn't talk. I also had a feeling they would probably get married soon. My friends asked me how I could be sure of that, and my response was that he was giving her everything she wanted in a relationship. I predicted that it would be soon just because of the way she had been moving, and I was right.

It was probably the end of February or beginning of March of 2023, when Susie 2 contacted me, and nonchalantly told me that she just got engaged. She didn't provide any details, and when I attempted to ask her how he proposed, she just moved on to something else. It was like she didn't want to tell me. It was very awkward, and I knew from that conversation that she was not going to have any more conversations with me about it or anything related to the wedding planning. And I was surely not going to be a bridesmaid. Twenty-five years of friendship and this was it.

Our conversations remained scarce, and her social media posts stayed the same. I went on with my life and continued to surround myself with my family and friends. I was hurting on the inside, but I still had hope that maybe one day things would go back to normal.

By the summer of 2023, I decided to attend a sorority conference. I always enjoy our conferences for the information learned and I would run into my sisters, who I attended college with, and from other chapters. One sister I was very familiar with, and we would often have conversations when we did run into each other. We would also speak about our school chapter and discuss homecoming activities each year.

I've never had a bad interaction with her until today. We were concluding our business meetings for the day, and everyone was waiting on their hotel shuttle. I ran across her and another one of my college sisters. I instantly went up to them with excitement because I was always happy to see them, but the aura was off. One of my sisters hugged me with open arms, while the other sister just gave me this mean mug like she didn't even want me to speak to her. It bothered my spirit because I have never done anything to this person a day in my life.

I knew I wasn't tripping because you can sense negative energy. I continued talking to my other sister, who was very welcoming, but this sister just stood there with an attitude. I ended the conversation and wished them well on the remainder of the trip.

While I was walking back to my hotel shuttle, I couldn't help but think, did Susie 2 tell her something negative about me? I mean Susie 2 would talk with her on a regular basis, and they were much closer than we were. Now, it was one thing to make subliminal messages about me on social media, but are you now telling the world that I am attacking you and your relationship? I really didn't know the answer, but my gut told me that was the case. It angered me, and at this point I had to just let the chips fall where they may. Several months passed with occasional phone calls here and there, but it was apparent that we would no longer be hanging out and that the once robust friendship was coming to an end.

The new year came, in and I received a bombshell. As, I was scrolling through my timeline on Facebook, and out of nowhere, I saw Susie 2's wedding pictures. I was flabbergasted and more hurt than ever. She had really gotten married, and I wasn't even included. I started crying again, and this time I just couldn't stop. I went to my daughter's room and showed her the pictures, and all she could do was shake her head. She told me she was sorry I was going through this and did not know what to say. At this point, I had to let everything out.

I sent Susie 2 a calendar request for an appointment to talk to her. I know that sounds crazy, but what do you do when your friend no longer has time for you? I ended up just calling her because I couldn't hold it in any longer. She answered the call, and I told her we needed to talk.

I was disappointed in seeing her wedding pictures on social media, and I didn't know how things had gotten off course for us. She told me she felt I wasn't happy for her and that every time she talked about her relationship, I didn't say much. I told her what could I say when she had already taken offense to my previous statements. She then goes on to say, that she had spoken to her friends about it, and she didn't know why I wasn't happy for her. So, you are telling people I am not happy for you? I was like, what I said was the truth, the first couple of months are the honeymoon stage, and let's see what happens.

That does not mean I was trying to be negative about your relationship. The truth is, you have been acting funny toward me since you started dating this guy. I brought up our Atlanta visit and how she responded to me at the vendors and when we went out for lunch before we left. I also brought up the fact that she stopped including me in stuff, and that every time we talked, she would rush me off the phone if he called. We were talking two to three times a day, almost daily, from now not talking days and weeks at a time. I went on to tell her that I have always supported her, and have never said anything negative about our friendship but, so saying that I am somehow attacking your relationship is farthest from the truth.

She then said I should have said something to her. So, are you trying to gaslight me? I just told you how I was feeling, and you said I should have said something, but at the same time, you told your friends that I wasn't supportive of your relationship. I started crying again, and I hated that I was so emotional, but it was so painful that this is where our relationship ended. She went on to say that her husband was a wonderful guy and that one day she hopes that I meet him. That she loved me and my daughter and hopes the best for us.

Just like that, it was over. She later sent me a text saying she was glad we were able to talk and that we have differing views about what happened in our friendship, and that's okay. She looked forward to having me and my daughter in her life. That was the last conversation I ever had with her.

So many emotions ran through me. I think I cried on and off for a whole month. I tried not to let my daughter know, but I reached out to my friends, and each time I would get emotional. They hated that I was going through this and really didn't know how to console me. To make matters worse, my grandma's birthday was coming up, and I always recognize that since she died, I get depressed during that time.

Once again, I reached out to my job's employee assistance program and requested a counselor. By this time in my life, I had a master's degree in counseling, and while I have the educational background, I realized I needed to seek counseling for myself through a licensed professional counselor. I was dealing with anxiety and depression, and while I could focus on self-care, I still needed to seek out treatment.

Emotionally I was not getting better, and I needed to take further action. If I had to compare it, it would be like asking a heart surgeon to operate on himself. You can't repair yourself with inadequate tools. I was able to connect with a counselor the following week. My counselor was a licensed clinical social worker. Our first visit, and as a matter of fact, all our visits were virtual. The first visit was the usual. I discussed the main reason why I was there and the emotions I was feeling.

For about 20 minutes, I just talked non-stop and cried. I explained how Susie 2 was a major part of my life and now that she is no longer there, I was having a hard time adjusting. Not only was I sad and angry, but I was being portrayed as this villain attacking her relationship. I was concerned that she was rushing into a relationship. I was seeing how her behavior was changing. Giving my opinion about the previous relationships never caused her to withdraw from me. My counselor repeated what I was saying and asked whether she had ever responded this way to me.

My response was no, as we were always up front with each other. I went on to tell her about the social media posts and how I knew that she was indirectly taking a jab at me. My counselor pointed out that social media can be good and bad, and that it was probably best to put it on pause or unfollow her so I wouldn't see what she was posting. We scheduled our next visit for the following week, and she gave me a homework assignment. She asked me to think about what I would say to her if I saw her in person.

Immediately after this session, I went on social media to unfollow her. I entered her name into the search bar, but nothing came up. That was strange. I went to my friend's list, and her name was there, but she had unfollowed me. I looked at the last time I had seen her posts, and it had been a while. I was no longer even her Facebook friend. Well dang! This made me even more upset. It was like I was never a part of her life.

Reality was sinking in, and it was sinking fast. I gave some thought to my counselor's question, but I really couldn't come up with anything. The only thing I could think to say if anyone asked was to respond that she had gotten married, and we hadn't spoken in a while. That's all I could think of. I mean, despite the circumstances, I wasn't trying to bash her to anyone, and I really did wish her the best.

The following week, I had my second visit, and my counselor Cassandra asked if I had come up with an answer. I informed her know that I could only think to respond that she had gotten married and that we hadn't spoken in a while. She advised me that the response was fine and that it would let anyone know that it was all you knew and that you had not spoken. If anyone wanted to dive deeper, my response could be even simpler by just responding that you haven't spoken to her. She asked me how often we met, and I said it was only once or twice a year. She went on to ask about our circle of friends and our encounters, and I said it was about the same. So, really, the likelihood that anyone was going to confront me about our relationship was very unlikely.

She then asked me why this relationship ending was so challenging for me. I sat there pondering for a couple of minutes before giving my response. It dawned on me that it was so hurtful because I felt that she was always someone I could count on and that we had a solid foundation. She, in essence, had abandoned me. I don't have a whole lot of friends, but I have a small tribe that I can count on. I really thought that she was a part of my tribe. I don't know if things would have been different if I had just kept my opinion to myself, or was it really time for our friendship to end? My counselor advised me that it is natural for friendships to dwindle often, meaning that as people grow in life, some relationships may not be able to withstand the test of time.

While others continue to grow because there is an understanding that life situations happen, and people make time for whom they want to make time for. What my friend was doing was a part of life. The issue is that you thought you would still be a part of it as her life grew. I told her that I have never been one to think that just because you are married, that all your friends should be married.

We all go through things at different times in our lives and therefore you can't count your single friend out, just because she isn't married. I was previously married, and I continued to have the same friends. As a matter of fact, she was one of those friends.

My counselor then asked me if I had given any thought to the idea that maybe she was letting her husband know what we discussed? If she told him, you had reservations about their relationship, he may not want her around you. I hadn't given much thought to that point, but thinking about it, if he thought I was against him, then it would be another reason for her not wanting to be friends with me or anyone. My counselor pointed out that we couldn't speculate anything, but she was trying to make me see things from both points of view.

For our next sessions, she wanted me to focus on what I was going to do now that the friendship had ended, and if there was a possibility of reconciliation. I had already given some thought to reconciliation, and I concluded that this was not an option. Not because I didn't cherish our friendship, but because I felt like my character was being assassinated because I gave her my opinion.

People have disagreements every day but don't go on a press tour and try to attack my character. I can't go along with that, but it still doesn't mean that I wish her ill will. Life is too short, and I can't hold grudges against anyone. I am just trying to figure out how to move past the bond that was built and is now gone.

For our next session, once again, my counselor asked me what I decided, and I told her reconciliation was not an option. I felt like I was being painted as the villain. I wished her and her family well, but I have accepted our friendship's demise. I could tell that people in our inner circle were acting differently toward me, and it was like they were taking her side. I just don't know how long I'll keep feeling this way.

The comparison was made that the end of the friendship felt like death to me. In death, you are mourning the loss of a loved one, and afterward, you question if you could have done anything differently to help the individual. From there, you are in this angry state because you no longer have that person in your life. I am basically grieving the loss of the friendship. I'm in disbelief that it happened, in pain emotionally, angry that it happened, depressed and lonely because the friendship is gone, working through my emotions and accepting what has happened. Not sure what stage I was in at that point, but I can say that I was actively trying to work through everything.

My counselor asked me what my life looked like in terms career, family, etc. I explained to her that I was actively working toward some professional goals, working on my health since I had to have a major surgery and focused on self-care. She asked what self-care looked like for me, and I said journaling, getting more sleep, taking mini vacations several times a year and exploring other career options. Our sessions continued, and I was able to accept what happened and move forward. Don't get me wrong, there are memories there, and every once and while, something triggers those memories. I often smile because as a whole it was once a great friendship. I still think about my former friend, and I pray that God is blessing her and her family with all of her wants and needs.

As you can see, my life has had some setbacks, and I realized that these setbacks could have easily broken me. However, I recognized that I needed to heal and recover from the environment and the things that had impacted me, to ensure I could have a better future. I want to explore trauma areas that many have dealt with and discuss ways to work toward recovery and healing. I am not just speaking from a place of what someone has said, but from a place I've been. I know firsthand what unhealed trauma looks like. We must decide how we are going to move forward in life, no matter the circumstances or what people say. With God's help and counseling, you will be able to attain that peace and equilibrium. You will be able to let go.

Chapter 4: The Trauma

Discussing the different types of traumas in this book is not done so to trigger anyone but it's done to bring awareness of the different types of trauma people may have experienced. Count yourself blessed if you have not experienced any form of trauma, but let's be empathetic toward others who may have been victimized. As we explore different types of traumas, unfortunately, most have been caused by someone you know. For some people, maybe it was a family member, a friend, or a coworker that you trusted and felt that they would never do anything to hurt you and that they would be there for you. The most common hurt is generally family hurt. Within my immediate circle or through people I know, almost everyone has experienced some kind of family trauma. What happens when you have a family member who has molested you or worse, your child? Individuals have experienced emotional and physical abuse from family members, and everyone seems to think it's not a big deal. Discussing these different forms of trauma, is to bring awareness and not to relive them.

To make matters worse, your family or friends may be aware of the trauma you have experienced; however, they have no empathy for the pain you have been caused or even acknowledge it. Growing up, one thing I would always hear people in my family say was, "The past is the past." And to be quite honest, it is, but that doesn't mean you are not going to have a memory of things that have happened. To think that you are somehow supposed to become numb to your experience is ridiculous. To make matters worse, what happens when the family chooses to keep what happened to you a secret? Telling what happens in this house stays in this house is the most abusive thing ever! You have experienced a family member or family friend's abusive behavior, and this behavior is often repeated. When, and if, you get the courage to tell someone, they can make you feel like you are making up a story, or they guilt you into thinking that you sharing your story you will get the family in trouble. This kind of behavior happens daily.

I recall watching this popular television show called, "Cops." It was a real-life reality show that took you behind the scenes of police in different cities as they answered 911 calls. During this episode, the cops were called to a home about a family disturbance. They never showed the faces of the family members, and I could only hear voices. My guess was it was to protect the victim's identity. It seems the mother's boyfriend called the police because his son was being touched inappropriately by his older brother, and he wanted the aggressor removed from the home. It was apparent that the man was not the oldest child's father. Because of the nature of the call and the ages of the children, ages 4 to 7, the police notified child protective services. I wondered what happened to this child that would make him molest his younger brother. So many questions came to mind, but I kept wondering whether the mother knew or suspected that the older child might only be mimicking behavior he'd experienced. And if she knew, what had she done to protect the other children and get help for the older child?

The police went off to the side to discuss the situation, and it was apparent to them the child was only doing what was done to him. This case required that two children be treated for abuse. What's a mother to do in this situation? Was she willing to give the oldest child up for the youngest child, even though both were victims? What was her behavior, and who did she allow around her children? Did she notice a change in the oldest child's behavior? I mean, as a mother if my child does something out of normal, I am asking questions. Sleeping all day or being withdrawn from activities are signs that something could be wrong.

I never knew the ending of this show, but it helped solidify my opinion that this type of trauma isn't unusual. I can't imagine how scarred both children would be, or what might happen if neither received counseling. In some cases, children are removed from the home, and unfortunately, in those cases, this leads to further abuse, and the cycle continues.

What if the oldest child did tell his mother that someone had touched him inappropriately, and she failed to do anything? You would be surprised how many people stay and put their children in danger because they don't want to change their lifestyle. Excuses I have personally heard are "I didn't want to leave because he was the main source of income," "I didn't know what I would do without him," "He takes care of me and the household, and I didn't know if my child was telling the truth." Better yet, they say, "I didn't want to be by myself and start over." That last part is a reality for many. A parent is choosing to stay with their partner who has abused one of their children because they do not want to be by themselves, or they want to keep up outward appearances. How does anyone sleep in the same bed with a partner who they know has sexually abused their child(ren)? Better yet, who would want to be with someone who they know has abused a child(ren)? I know the questions are hard, but what's even harder is the pain that child(ren) are experiencing because of the abuse.

I had a close friend who had a family member who gave her daughter up when her daughter confided in her and told her that her boyfriend was touching her. The child was in elementary school, and her mother had moved her boyfriend into her home. Not sure how long he had been molesting the child, but what was certain was that she went to her mom for protection. As can happen, this mother decided it was easier to give up her daughter and stay with the man. To be more specific, my friend said the little girl was sent to stay with her grandmother. I asked if she had received any counseling or if she had seen her mom, and I was told that the mom said she didn't know if the girl was telling the truth, so she didn't report it to the police. Everyone just stepped up to help the grandmother take care of the child, she said, but I was left feeling certain that that child was feeling abandoned by her mother.

People don't want to discuss what happens when you realize a family member is the abuser. Families can make the victim feel bad or accuse them of being dishonest to protect the family name. We know this does not help anything because usually the abuser goes on to abuse someone else. It's a cycle that keeps repeating itself, and the victims are traumatized for life.

What if you decide my child is telling the truth, but your resolution is not to report it, and you send your child away to stay with a relative, or even worse, allow them to be placed in foster care? In some cases, the abuser is sent off to stay with another relative, but there is no attempt to correct the behavior. The last scenario is very common, and often it leads to other forms of abuse. Everyone is aware of the situation and what has taken place but there have been no repercussions for the abuser and no attempt at any kind of treatment.

While you may think you are keeping them from being abused or doing the abuse you may be opening the door for something else to happen. Are you thinking about your child at that moment and what type of environment you are sending them to? You are uprooting them from an environment they have learned to adapt to, and in most situations, put them in another environment with complete strangers. The child is normally thinking it's my fault this happened because I said something. Is there any counseling involved to help with coping skills, or do you just send them away?

So much to upload as an adult, but imagine all this happening to a child. Children depend on their parents to protect and provide for them. Imagine the resentment and lack of trust a child develops once they realize that their parent(s) are not going to look out for their best interest or better yet even protect them. It would make any child have trust and commitment issues as the people they relied on the most let them down, and in some cases, may have allowed these horrible acts of abuse to happen. Anybody would have trust issues, especially if the main people they were supposed to be able to trust failed at their job.

Sexual abuse, just like any other form of abuse, will leave individuals mistrusting others and doubting themselves. They could be triggered by someone stroking their hair, touching them on the shoulder, or even by someone being too close to them. The key would be to identify those triggers and work through processes to avoid or get out of uncomfortable situations.

However, we all know that life happens, therefore if you avoid human interaction, how does that help you to develop mentally and spiritually? For some people, these triggers might leave them in a state of paralysis. They may think they have totally blocked the previous behavior, only to find out that they can be easily triggered. Those memories eventually resurface, and when they do does, it may be an inappropriate setting or time. It could be something as simple as attending a party, and one of the attendees' physical appearances may remind you of your abuser. Are you going to leave the party or stay?

Identifying your triggers is necessary to work toward resolutions that will help in human interaction. For instance, if you're uncomfortable with someone hugging you or getting in your personal space, it would be beneficial to extend your hand for a handshake instead. This will let them know that this is your preferred method of physical touch. If the person persists, as some people can be, you can reiterate your preference. Setting boundaries are a must for your emotional well-being.

We must also be mindful of the places and people we encounter. If someone's behavior is questionable, avoid them or limit the access they have to you. Letting people know if they have done something to offend or trigger you is vital. People don't automatically know your story or your trauma, it's your job to share, if you feel led to, or to set boundaries for how people approach you. Pull them to the side, express how you are feeling and be open to the conversation. It's our job to determine what works for us. Take care of you.

Chapter 5: Mental And Physical Abuse

In addition to sexual abuse, there is also mental and physical abuse. Some say mental abuse is the most dangerous because the individuals are subjected to words that demean, belittle and strip away their self-esteem. Telling someone that they are stupid, slow or that they will never amount to anything leaves lifelong scars. People may not see the damage with mental abuse, but it's there, nevertheless. When your self-esteem is affected, you may feel worthless. Or what happens when people comment on your physical appearance and laugh at you because you don't meet their physical appearance expectations. Commenting on an individual's weight, skin color or hair texture in a negative way can cause them to have self-esteem issues. People never forget how you made them feel, and the saying "actions speak louder than words" can be challenged. Positive affirmations and words of encouragement speak life into individuals and situations.

The American Psychological Association defines physical abuse as a deliberate, aggressive, or violent behavior by one person toward another that results in bodily injury. Physical abuse may involve actions such as choking, kicking, punching, shaking or beating. In some cases, physical abuse may lead to a traumatic brain injury or even death. How can an adult injure a child to the point of bruises, broken bones or even death? Or better yet, how can an adult do these things to another adult?

The common denominator in all forms of abuse is that someone is attempting to gain control or dominance over another person. It's about power for the abuser. Individuals in any of these settings are often scared to vocalize their opinions, make any sudden movement and freely live in their own home. Just like with sexual abuse, the excuses are the same and the cycle just keeps repeating itself.

According to National Coalition Against Domestic Violence, national statistics note that 20 people per minute are physically abused by an intimate partner in the United States. This averages to about 10 million women and men per year. According to Forbes magazine (May 15, 2020), 80% of Americans have experienced emotional abuse. Fear, finances, loneliness, low self-esteem and resources are key factors in why individuals choose to stay in their abusive environments.

To make matters worse, people feel guilty about leaving, especially if their pastor or other spiritual leader tells them to stay in their abusive situation and pray for their partner because they are supposed to forgive. Well, we all know forgiveness is about helping us to move forward, but that doesn't mean that you should remain in that abusive environment. Being a good Christian is not dependent upon your staying in an abusive relationship. God or any higher power would not want you or your children to be in a situation where you are being mistreated. That's a whole different story that we will discuss later.

If children are involved in any kind of abusive relationship, a parent has the responsibility to protect and provide for their child. Any move you take to protect your child, you must know that God will provide. There is nothing easy about this situation, nor about situations like this, but the priority must be whether I am doing what is best for my child or children. Allowing a molester or abuser to remain in your home or for you to remain in their home cannot be an option. How do you think a child would feel knowing that the abuser was chosen over them? I've heard people say they have no choice but to stay due to the situation. But know that remaining is a decision. Situations like this can lead to resentment, isolation and in some cases rebellion.

Some parents know what's happening but choose to ignore it. Then when the child misbehaves, they act like they don't know what triggers that behavior. You take a blind eye to what happened to your child, and you then blame the child for their misbehavior. No one takes responsibility, and no one helps the child. Imagine your parent choosing to ignore the fact that you have been abused, and then to make matters worse, they act like they don't understand or know why your behavior has changed. While ignoring the abuse is horrible, blaming the child for the behavior of the adult can be worse.

Young girls are often blamed for "acting grown," or trying to entice the adult abuser. You must be kidding me! Why is a grown adult looking at a child sexually? And more importantly why are you not questioning their behavior or better yet removing them or yourself and child(ren) from the home? What type of individual have you brought into your home around your children? To blame the child and not acknowledge what has happened to them is a cowardly act. This is a memory they will never forget. Telling them that "the past is the past" is not easy to get over. Also, that abuser will continue to abuse others if his or her crime goes unreported. No one seems to consider that, if left untreated, most people repeat the same behaviors. That means that the abuser just goes on to their next victim. This should be something that we should make every attempt to avoid.

Parents who physically abuse their children like to say, "my parents spanked me, and I turned out fine," or a "hard head makes a soft butt." You are hitting your child so hard that they are bruised, or you break their bones, and you answer that you experienced it, so get over it. At some point, the cycle of abuse needs to stop. We are in the

21st century, and what we should now know and understand is that discipline does not equate to physical abuse.

In situations where the adult is being abused, the abuser often isolates them from their family and friends. Attending family functions such as cookouts, baby showers, weddings, birthday parties, funerals, or holiday gatherings is a thing of the past as the abuser takes control of their personal lives. The need to keep you away from people who will possibly sway you and help you leave is their objective, and they often use intimidation and isolation to keep you in line.

Why would anyone stay in a situation where they are made to feel guilty when they want to spend time with people who have supported and loved them? There are multiple reasons, but some people don't even realize that they are in an abusive relationship because the behaviors they have witnessed in their immediate environment may be considered normal or they lack the self-esteem to start over. In short, they witnessed it firsthand and believe this is normal.

Generational curses are real, and people raised in abusive households often end up with the same type of spouse or significant other because they are looking for what is familiar. Imagine someone saying, "Even though your dad beat me, he still took care of his family." It is like you have been told that if they pay the bills, the abuse is okay. They stay in the household despite the fights, bruises and broken bones. What is normal for you may not be normal for someone else, and therefore, we can't conclude such. Some abusers often use finances to remain in control. Leaving their partner dependent on them, which allows them to stay in control, is a harmful situation.

But the individual must reach that point where enough is enough, and they want to do something different. Children don't have that option as they are dependent on the parents to take care of them. How many emergency room visits will it take for you to decide to do something different? Or better yet, how are you going to keep explaining the physical bruises? At some point, it is not even going to make sense to you and when that happens, is when you will realize that you must do something different. Or it could come from the mouth of a babe. How will you answer your child(ren) when they ask you why can't we leave? To make matters worse, what if your child starts to display behaviors similar to your abuser? It's okay to start over and more importantly, it's okay to make yourself and your children a priority. People start over every day, and the only way to work towards it is to make the decision you want a change. As humans we are not responsible for someone's opinion about themselves or their actions.

We are, however, responsible for our own actions. When you look in the mirror what are you striving for? How do you want your child(ren) to see you? If you are not living the life you desire, then it is up to you to make some changes. Eventually, you must decide if you want to live to see another day and if you want the opportunity to live your life more abundantly.

Make a plan, write it down, and take the necessary steps to start making the changes necessary for your life. Utilize your family and friends for your support. Take advantage of community resources that help with trauma, job assistance and training, and relocation. For a while you may not feel comfortable, however as you work towards your goals, your situation and emotional state will improve. Material things can be replaced, however your child's innocence cannot. Evaluate what is important in your life and the life you created.

Chapter 6: Parental Trauma

What happens when an absentee parent (mother or father) abandons you and reappears in your adulthood as if nothing happened? Or what about parents who mentally, physically and emotionally drain you but still expect you to show them respect? Or the parent who ignores you but is there for other siblings or other children? There are so many scenarios that we can address. One thing is certain, growing up and getting the love and care needed from both parents can be difficult. And those difficulties can affect how you act and respond, unless you recognize the issues and work at providing something to your offspring that you yourself didn't receive.

Being related by blood does not make you family; it is a statement that is 100% accurate. Let's consider absentee parents. Some have missing parents because of illness, incarceration, molestation, accidents or even war. I'm including in this discussion, children removed from their parents' home for a number of reasons, because no matter the reason, the parent is still absent.

While those situations may be different, and we can understand if the parent thought raising them in a different environment would be better, the children are still abandoned and have little or no relationship with their parents.

Many of us know people raised by someone other than a parent. I have even heard stories of a parent staying in the same neighborhood as their child, and they ignore them. Imagine growing up and being told this is your mother or father, only to encounter them and have them pretend you don't exist. It takes a cold-hearted individual to do something like that, and there are a lot of cold-hearted individuals out there. I know this because, as I discussed earlier, that's my story. So, I know the trauma this can cause.

In certain situations, stepping away from the child may be the best course of action. Some people aren't responsible enough to raise a child, may be incapable of doing so or they lack the desire to become parents. They never wanted the responsibility, and even after having the child, they lack the motivation to step into their parental role.

Our society teaches that we will go from child to adult to parents and then grandparents. However, not everyone desires to be a parent or grandparent. Therefore, when an adult with this mindset becomes a parent, they often run away from the responsibility.

I'm reminded of the different reality television shows where people find their long-lost family members, and the whole time, they are less than 20 minutes away. You mean to tell me no one knew about this child? To make matters worse, family will often make excuses for the absentee parent and will tell you to get over it because plenty of people didn't have their parents. Are you kidding me? Just because they are your family doesn't mean what they did was right. Reappearing in a child's life after they are grown is not okay, and people shouldn't make excuses for you. Family or not, it is wrong. I mean, you just act like nothing happened and don't even try to explain or apologize.

Have you heard about the parents who went to the store to get a pack of cigarettes or a loaf of bread, and they disappeared until you were grown? Could be a TV storyline except it happens all the time. Sometimes they don't even give you a lame excuse, they just leave. Then other family members have the nerve to tell you that you need to respect them and honor them because they are the parent, when they do decide to show up.

Respect goes both ways, and simply showing up and saying I am here now does not erase the fact that you have been absent for their entire life. Biologically, yes, they are your parents, but that is where it stops; for your whole life, you have been absent. What happened to honoring your children and providing for them? Just producing or giving birth to a child does not obligate the child to a lifetime of taking care of you. Just as children are supposed to honor their parents, parents also should honor their children. Giving birth to your child and showing back up when they are grown and traumatized does not give anyone the right to expect their child to just pretend like everything was just peachy.

What about the parent who was addicted to drugs for most of their child's life and after 20 years or more, finally makes the decision to get clean? Don't get me wrong, any form of addiction is hard to break, and anyone who has had a family member or friend addicted to drugs, knows firsthand that they are constantly looking for that first hit that they will never get again.

Most end up losing their homes, jobs, friends, family, and most importantly, themselves. It is a hard pill to swallow, however, for most children, they will never understand how a drug or gambling addiction made their parent abandon them. For some, they may have started out with that parent in the home, and therefore, they have those memories. On the other hand, the parent may have never been involved because they were actively using drugs while the child was conceived, and the child was taken once the parent delivered.

If you were lucky enough to have one parent who was stable in your life, then count it as a blessing. However, some individuals had to face the fact that both of their parents were addicts and thus missing from their lives.

Most of us know it's hard to discuss the low points in your life, but if you expect yourself or the other person to heal, you have to acknowledge what happened. Not doing so hinders the repair of the relationship. Imagine suffering abuse because you had to be placed in foster care because your parent(s) were strung out, but they don't want to talk about it because it is in the past. Your emotional and often physical scars are still present even if your parent doesn't want to talk about them. While some may find it hard, some individuals choose to love their parents from a distance because even though they may love you, they can't do life with someone who chooses not to acknowledge their feelings.

Life is hard for everyone, but you must decide how to live your life. Plenty of parents aren't rich, but they are able to provide love, wisdom, a home and support to their child. Just walking away from your responsibility because things got tough isn't an excuse. Not acknowledging or telling someone they don't have a right to be upset or even disappointed because it's your family member is a bit ridiculous. People have a right to be angry and even disappointed. You don't have the right to discredit how they feel. Family or not, you shouldn't make excuses for them not doing right by their biological child(ren). Keep your insensitive comments to yourself and stop making excuses for people who willingly walked away. Even when a person finds a family member(s) they didn't know existed, our comments can turn them away.

Let's face it, would you want to go to an environment where you were hurt? Or better yet, a hostile environment where individuals are trying to make you feel bad about your feelings? It's toxic, and no one is going to be around people who make them feel bad. While I was attending a high school graduation gathering for a family member, a senior family member, who happened to be a distant cousin, told me I was bougie and that I acted like my family wasn't good enough to come around. This same family member was a Facebook friend, and she mentioned that I had time to travel and do other things but not see the family. This same family member has never been to my house even though we stay in the same city and every time we did interact was because I attended a family gathering or when I came to her house. She never made any attempts to communicate outside of the family gatherings, never offered any congratulatory remarks for any of my accomplishments or my child's accomplishments, and better yet, doesn't even have my phone number. But I am the person who must reach out to her and the family, even though they don't reach out to me.

To make matters worse, this same family member who just tried to insult me, tries to double down on her comments, once I advise her that I am not going around negativity, and it works both ways. Her response was, "Oh I was just playing, I didn't mean any harm." You really tried to gaslight me and think I wouldn't respond to you. Now, why would I want to be around someone with this negative energy?

Unfortunately, this scenario is becoming way to common. But what happens when your parents' divorce and suddenly, the non-custodial parent completely stops seeing their child, or the parent who has primary custody refuses to abide by the court-ordered child custody agreement and keeps you from seeing the other parent? This is a lot to take in, as a child is depending on their parents to do the right thing.

However, because there is often so much animosity from the divorce proceedings or separation, some parents choose to take out their frustration on the child and decide they are going to punish the other parent by not physically or financially supporting the child. Or the parent decides that I am going to keep the child(ren) from the parent that is not in the household because they want to be spiteful and get back at the other parent because the relationship ended. Phone calls and visits just stop suddenly, and no one steps up to do the right thing.

This isn't the 60s, meaning today's custody cases are more about what is best for the child. The courts will work to resolve conflicts when both people involved are not focused on the child's well-being. A parent who chooses not to comply with the custody agreement can be legally held responsible for their actions. Therefore, being absent from your child's life really is a decision you make.

Another situation to consider is what happens to a child when one parent remarries and forgets their children from a previous relationship. I am using the word "forget,", but how can one just forget they have a child? They will enter a new relationship and take on the responsibility of taking care of someone else's children and abandon their own biological children. I wouldn't' want a partner who doesn't take care of their children, but some individuals feel that if their household is taken care of, they don't care about anything else.

Imagine staying in the same county and your child(ren) attend the same school as their stepsiblings, and your parent is showing up to games and PTA meetings for someone else's child(ren). They don't interact with you at all and act as if you are a stranger. For some it's a reality, and for any child, this can be a painful experience. I would question my partner about their absence from their children's life and vocalize my expectation for him/her to take care of their responsibility.

We cannot make people do anything, but let's not make lame excuses for an absentee parent who does nothing for their child(ren). Also, if they did it to their children, what makes you think they wouldn't do it to you and your children if things ended badly? In addition, the stepparent would even make excuses for the absentee parent, and would say things like, "they pay their child support." While the parent may be paying child support, it does not replace them from physically and emotionally being in their child's life.

To make matters worse, some adults will question the child's paternity once they are in the new relationship. Now, the parent didn't have these questions when you two were together, but now that they've moved on, they start to say things like, "He doesn't really look like me." Make it make it sense to me that a child you have taken care of since birth, but suddenly you are not sure of their paternity, so therefore you just stop taking care of the child(ren). Instead of being an adult and getting a paternity test administered initially, you just ghost your child. Did you really have doubts about paternity, or did you decide, 'If I am not with the mother, then I am not going to take care of my child?" How can you take the responsibility of taking care of someone else's child and you refuse to take care of your own?

This was an issue I had to deal with personally. My child is now 24 years old, and as adults, we discuss how this has affected her. My daughter's father and I dated during college and after college, off and on. After college, our relationship, well, at least I thought, grew stronger. We spent time together, discussed each other's dreams and aspirations, and I supported him emotionally. During our time together, I got pregnant with my daughter. I was in shock, which I don't know why, because that's a chance you take when you are having unprotected sex, but I was still in shock because it was not something I wanted at that time in my life. I was 23 years old and not married. That was not something I planned, and to be honest, I was beyond scared to have a child. Being a parent is not an easy task, and I knew that I wanted something better for my child whenever that time came.

When I realized that I was pregnant after taking several pregnancy tests and my doctor confirmed that I was, I confided in my daughter's dad. I did not know how he would react because he was working towards his goals. However, I was confident that he would react positively. We were both adults, and I had supported him in every aspect of his life up until this point. When I called him, we started out with our normal pleasantries, and I told him that I went to the doctor and that I was pregnant. For several seconds, there was silence. What happened next caught me totally off guard. He asked me how far along

I was and then proceeded to tell me that this wasn't something either one of us planned, and that it would be best that I have an abortion. Not the answer I was expecting, and I was hurt that this was the response. He then tells me that an abortion should cost about $300, that he knew someone who had one, and that basically it was no big deal. I, he said, would get over it. I was speechless. I told him that while this was not planned, I wasn't sure what to do and that I just needed to think about the situation and call him back. We ended the call, and I went into panic mode. I wasn't expecting him to just to say something like that to me. He seemed so heartless.

I confided in a close male friend, who just happens to be my daughter's godfather, and we discussed, of course, how it is literally a miracle to get pregnant. We discussed that either way there was no promise that we were going to be together no matter what the decision was; however, there was a possibility that I may never have the opportunity to have another child.

I went to see my obstetrician for my first prenatal visit, and we had a consultation after my exam. My doctor was an older gentleman, and he looked over my chart, and he commented that he didn't see that I was married. No offense was taken to his comment, as this was something I was thinking about the whole time. He asked how involved the father was and what did I plan to do if he chose not to be involved with me or the child. My response was that he had asked me to abort the child and that he was not interested in being a parent. Scared and nervous, were my current feelings, and I really was not 100% sure of what I was going to do exactly.

My doctor went on to tell me that he had been practicing for quite a while, and that he had patients who, unfortunately, were in similar situations. Many were optimistic that the father would step up once they saw the child and in almost 50% of more of those cases, the fathers did exactly what they said they would do, which is nothing. He told me that if I made the decision to have the child that the reality may be that I may be doing it alone, and he reminded me that having a child is a blessing. My doctor told me to pray about it, and to let his office know my decision so they could plan the next steps. I left the office still not 100% certain, but I knew that I had to make a decision that was best for me.

Just like anything else in my life, I went to the Lord in prayer. I asked for forgiveness, and I asked him to help me make the right decision. I spoke with a family friend who happened to be a pastor, and I continued to seek the Lord. After about a week or so, I knew I could not have an abortion just to please a man. It was not right for me, and the probability of me getting pregnant again was something I did not know and wasn't willing to take a chance. I called my daughter's father and told him my decision. This poor excuse for a human being, responds to my decision and informs me that he wants absolutely nothing to do with me or the child.

I informed him that was fine, however I did not make this child by myself, therefore, he would be supporting the child financially. Our call ended and I think I cried for days. His response to me and his unborn child was a total shocker. What was truly disappointing is that this man grew up without a father and had always talked about being there for his children when the time came. Not being with me was disappointing, but I could accept that. Rejecting your child was something that I couldn't understand, but just like anything else, I knew that God would make a way and be there for me.

The next several months when I should have been enjoying my pregnancy, I was battling depression and trying to prepare to be a single parent. I was reading books, having discussions with my family and friends who already had children and making sure I was going to all my doctor visits. God is so merciful, that during my whole pregnancy, my daughter's now godfather, called me almost every, single day to check up on me and to pray with me. I continued to work, go to church and spend time with my family. Even though I was depressed, I knew I was carrying a blessing.

I was in my last trimester of my pregnancy and suddenly, my daughter's father started reaching out to me. I wish I could say it was a positive interaction, but it wasn't. He sends me this email and tells me that he has had time to think, and that he wants to be in his child's life. However, he doesn't want to be with me, and that he was preparing to marry the woman he truly loved. Are you kidding me?

You contact me to antagonize me and to bring even more stress to my pregnancy that you have been absent from? What a jerk, and what did he think my response was going to be. He continued to send me emails, saying that his fiancée, whoever this person was, wanted to meet me. So, you abandon me during my pregnancy, email me only to really say you are getting married to a person that I didn't even know existed, and you decided you want to be there for the child. I didn't comment on the fiancé or pending marriage, but I let him know my due date, and we can discuss things once the child gets here.

Fast forward, my water breaks while I am in the shower, and I really start to freak out. I call my cousin, who had taken Lamaze classes with me, and let him know that it was time for the baby. Luckily, my hospital bag was already packed, and once I called my doctor, I went to the hospital. I got there around 11 a.m. and once my doctor checked me, I had dilated three centimeters. My doctor informed me it was just a matter of time. We begin the process of contacting everyone to let them know I was in labor, and my cousin asked a very important question. Do you want me to call her dad? I didn't even have him on the list because he was missing in action during the whole pregnancy.

Even though he had reached out via email I wasn't confident that he truly wanted to be involved. But as usual, I had to do the right thing, so I told my cousin to call him and let him know. I said to myself, he is not going to come, and I could at least say he was informed. To my surprise, he answered the phone, and my cousin explained who he was and the reason for the call. Before I knew it, the address of the hospital was being provided and the phone number to my room. After the call, my cousin and I discussed if he was going to come, and I replied that I had no confidence that he would due to his absence.

We went about practicing breathing techniques and the nurses checked me every so often to see how far I was dilating. My cousin and my daughter's godmother stayed with me the whole time and talked with me. The next thing you know, my daughter's dad reappeared out of nowhere, and walked into my hospital room, like nothing happened.

The next action was total disbelief, as he placed his hand on my shoulder and asked me if I was okay. Did you seriously just walk into my hospital room after disappearing during my whole pregnancy and act like nothing happened? All eyes were on him, and no one could believe he was there. He spoke with my cousin and friend and proceeded to sit down in the hospital chair. At that time, my cousin advised me that they were going to get something to eat and come back. While in the room, he didn't have really anything to say and just watched television. After about two hours, my cousin and friend returned.

By then I had dilated about eight centimeters, and my delivery was almost here. The nurses told me that only two people could be in the room and to let them know who was going to be there. This dude walks to my bedside and tells me that he would like to be in the room to witness his daughter being born. Are you kidding me? I know, I am using this expression a lot, but I really was in disbelief. My cousin looked at me and wanted to know what I was going to do. I told my daughter's father that I did not want him in the room, however I would allow him to stay in the room, as it was the right thing to do. My friend, who had supported me during the whole pregnancy, stepped out of the room, while my cousin coached me and videotaped the delivery. I couldn't believe it, after three pushes, my daughter was born. Her dad, of course, was of no support, as he was just there. To make matters worse, once the nurses cleaned her off, he held her before I did. The man who didn't want the child held her before the actual mother did. As I watched him hold her, I could see him counting her toes, fingers and looking at her ear. It was like he was looking for similarities.

My beautiful daughter was here, and I was so thankful to God for a healthy child. The interactions after my daughter's birth were even more disappointing. Her father signed her birth certificate, advocated for her to have his last name, and advised me that he would help. I was released from the hospital and started my bonding journey with my daughter. Her dad started calling and coming by to see her, alone. I still had no idea who this fiancé was, and he never mentioned her again. At any rate, I was starting to prepare to go back to work, and, of course, I had already added her to my health coverage and picked out a daycare. I spoke with her father about her expenses, and due to his absence from my pregnancy and an unwillingness to come to terms with a child support agreement, I filed for child support through the court system.

His next action was disappointing but not surprising. He filed for full custody of my daughter, you know the daughter he didn't want and asked for a blood test. Now, I realize that people do things just out of spite and to hurt you and that is what he did. I willing gave him the blood test, as I had nothing to hide. However, as he is an attorney, I wondered why he would sign a legal document, like the birth certificate, and then question the paternity? Also, who petitions to take a newborn child from their willing and capable mother? At any rate, I continued to do the right thing, and we went to court where I was awarded full custody, and he received visitation.

I mean, this guy was so confident in himself that he represented himself in court even though he had zero experience in child custody cases. The judge, however, saw through the antics and based his decision on the facts, advising us both that two professional people should do what is best and co-parent for the child's sake.

I know, it's taking a while to get to the point, but I just wanted to lay the foundation. Fast forward, my daughter is three years old and as parents we are cordial, and he is abiding by his custody agreement. Every other weekend he would come and get his daughter, and this went on without a hitch. However, this situation changed when he got married. To my surprise, he married a woman who is divorced with three children. How can you go from not wanting your one child to marrying someone with three children and taking care of them? Suddenly, where we once were cordial, he can barely speak and communicates primarily through texts and emails. To make matters worse, he begins focusing on other areas of his life and did not consider his child to be a priority.

I witnessed this at my daughter's fourth birthday party, where I invited him. At this point, I was just trying to be cordial and include him. Well, he shows up to the party late with his wife and three stepchildren. The whole time, he doesn't interact with his daughter and gives his attention to his stepchildren. When it is time to sing happy birthday, cut her cake and open gifts, we learn that he didn't even bring her a gift. Not even a $5 doll baby, which, at her age, all she wanted to do was open something. Her godfather and my cousin looked at me in a state of shock, like Who doesn't bring a gift for their child to a birthday party?" I wish I could say this was just an isolated incident, but it only got worse as she got older and was involved in activities.

As my daughter started to participate in sports, clubs, organizations and activities at church, her father could never make the time to see her. As a matter of fact, he would tell her he couldn't come because he was too busy. Now, mind you, he only saw her every other weekend. But every football game and other sport activities he made an effort for others especially his other children. As she got older, I really couldn't say anything, but my daughter was so used to him not being there that she just programmed herself not to be disappointed. Every accomplishment my child earned, he would be the first person to take credit when in reality he didn't help her in any way, shape, or form.

During her senior year in high school, she participated in my sorority's debutante cotillion. The cotillion was a huge deal as it is a formal event, and it is basically an introduction to society. Several rehearsals are involved, and the parents are expected to escort their daughters into the ball as they are introduced. As soon as my daughter was accepted, she immediately contacted her father to let him know the rehearsal dates.

You know this joker told her he couldn't commit to the rehearsals because her little brother normally had baseball practices on Sundays. You mean to tell me that the mom couldn't take him to practice and that you couldn't miss a couple of them? I mean my daughter could count on both hands how many games you have been to for her over the course over 15 years, and you have never taken her to any of her soccer, basketball or track and field practices. My daughter was disappointed yet again, but as always when she looked on his social media pages it was like she didn't even exist because he only posted the other children.

Even when she attended college, he made a point to tell everyone she was there and to brag about her accomplishments. However, he only visited her in college twice, once to drop her off and once on her graduation day.

As an adult, my daughter confided in me that it was hurtful to her growing up, seeing her father be present for other children and not her. As a matter of fact, she said that a lot of times when she did visit with him, he didn't interact with her. Her dad purchased a home and built it from the ground up. However, when she went to visit, she had to share a room. I understand it's normal to share rooms growing up but by this age, she was a teenager not a little child. When she asked her dad about having her own space, he told her she could sleep in the guest room. Was she a part of the family or a guest? Every other family member had their own room, but she was considered a guest.

She made several attempts to speak with her dad about her feelings, and each time he gaslighted her. One time, he told her, "The phone works both ways" when she asked why he doesn't call to check on her. The relationship she desired, did not exist and it wasn't because of me or her but because of this lack of effort from her father. The opportunity for it to grow was there, but his desire was not.

I am so thankful that I was involved in her in activities, taught her about Jesus Christ and more importantly, placed individuals in her life who would pour into her. To this very day, she thanks me for choosing her godfather, as he has filled the father gap and stepped up. It is still painful to her to not have that relationship with her dad, but she reminds herself that relationships work both ways. I could easily blame the stepmother for his lack of interest in her, but the truth of the matter is, it is not her fault, and he never wanted his child in the first place. He did the bare minimum to keep up appearances, and that minimum prevented him from developing a close relationship with his firstborn child.

Some situations don't fit any of these scenarios, and some parents choose not to be involved simply because the child is no longer in the same household with them. When that child gets older or if they encounter friends or family members who have both parents present, they wonder why that absent parent(s) wasn't present in their lives. To make matters worse, the absentee parent may feel that it is the child's responsibility to seek them when they get older and become adults. That's right, you heard me. They want the child, that they abandoned, to come looking for them.

Some parents keep the child away from the parent who is not in the household and will do everything they can to keep them away. It is a hard pill to swallow however to learn that there was nothing in the way of that parent being in your life other than they didn't want to be inconvenienced or there was always something more important than them. However, the absentee parent's demand for respect simply because they are the parent is narcissistic because they didn't honor their end of the bargain by raising and pouring into the child. Children don't ask to be born, and the argument that the child who never asked to be here in the first place owes you something is a crock.

According to Ephesians 6, verses 1-4 (New International Version,), it states "children, obey your parents in the Lord, for this is right. Honor your father and mother, which is the first commandment with a promise, so that it may go well with you and that you may enjoy long life on the earth." Verse 4 continues, "Fathers, do not exasperate your children; instead, bring them up in the training and instruction of the Lord." When we look at the word train, according to the dictionary, it means to teach a particular skill or type of behavior through practice and instruction over a period. For those individuals who call themselves parents, if you are not doing right by your own child, why would you think that God or your higher being is not going to hold you responsible? It's okay to accept someone else's child, but it's not okay to abandon your own child in the process of doing this.

What about the scenario where the parent(s) leave you with a family member to get themselves together? They may have relocated to get a better job or to go to school so they could take care of you and themselves. In life, we know situations happen that cause individuals to get off track, and sometimes you simply need to start over. There is no harm in admitting that a refocus is needed if you are going to improve your circumstances. The issue is that the temporary agreement stretches into a couple of months, and the next thing you know, it's' been a couple of years. Their financial situation has improved and so has their living condition; however, you are still being taken care of by other family members or remain in foster care. To make matters worse, the said parent or parent(s) bring another child into this world, and they are taking care of them with no problem, while you are still left in the care of others. The excuse might be that they didn't want to pull them from the environment they were in because that is what they were used to, but that environment was only supposed to be temporary. You can now take care of your child, and you choose not to.

That child can visibly see that your circumstances have improved and that you now have other child(ren) you are supporting. What is your explanation for telling the child, I raised your siblings, but I couldn't raise you? Abandonment from a parent who was fully capable of taking care of you and providing for you is no different from a parent who simply decided that they didn't want to take care of you.

And taking care of a child is more than just providing money and being there. Some parents may be present but are emotionally abusing the child. Every chance they get, they remind you that you ruined their dreams and plans. They recall the opportunities they had to turn down because they had to take care of you. They make comments like, "I couldn't go to college because I had you," or "I wanted to take that job, but I had no one to take care of you." It is always something they could have done, but they had you, and because of that, you get blamed for everything that is not going right in their life.

Some people might argue that at least you were not given up for adoption or homeless, which would be correct. But who wants to be blamed their whole life for merely existing when they had no control over existing? It was not the child's fault that you had sex and that you became pregnant because of it. What were you doing to prevent this from happening? It's a bit ludicrous to blame an innocent child for something that could have been prevented.

Once the child finally leaves the household, they have no desire to return. Most people would understand that, but the emotionally abusive parent will guilt-trip the child(ren) and tell them they owe them because they took care of them. What exactly does a child owe a parent when they did not ask to be born? You were a parent, and it was your responsibility to care for this child. Most children who experienced a positive upbringing go out of their way to do things for their parents when they are financially able. But it's not their obligation to do so. It is not an "I owe you" situation because you birthed and raised them. That's what you were supposed to do.

Chapter 7: Relationship Trauma

Let's face it, the season for some of our relationships has ended. When the season has passed it normally means that maybe you and that individual no longer share the common interests or you have outgrown each other. What's hard for us to understand is when the season for family relationship end. That's a hard pill to swallow.

Family members are often some of our best friends and we stay with them through thick and thin. We never question the friendship because we have never had a reason to. But living by the code "that, "blood is thicker than water," is wrong as family members often don't respect and honor our friendships. I mean you could open a business or even write a book and instead of family members supporting my efforts, they will complain about everything from the cost of items to your logo's graphic design. And if the business is a financial success and you choose to elevate your lifestyle, prepare for the green, jealous monsters to appear. Moving to a new house or out of the neighborhood doesn't mean you don't appreciate or forgot where you came from.

What's wrong with moving to another community? My hometown, for instance, really has not seen much growth and development, since the 30 years that I left. It is still a small town where everyone pretty much knows everybody. A handful of shops have opened and closed. Most people, travel outside of the city for jobs, and remain in the area due to lower cost of living and family ties. However, there really isn't much there. For me, my visits are less frequent and short, because I only go to visit family members for the day, and when I am there, there really aren't any recreational activities immediately available. Also, for me it is a reminder that I was the poor kid who didn't have that great small-town upbringing.

Honestly, the environment some of us grew up in could be the same place that will get you killed today. Gang violence and drugs may have been very prominent in the area you had to grow up in and it is just not safe for you to be there.

As well as, my success doesn't mean I need to be the ATM machine for the rest of the family. Some family members and even friends will drain you financially. It is always an issue, or something is always coming up and when the issue arises the first person, they call is you to bail them out. While in the beginning it may be $50 here and there, the next thing you know the demands are in the hundreds or more. Eventually, you stop making withdrawals from the ATM because you realize that, financially, you just can't keep doing it, or more importantly, no one should be depending on your money.

Suddenly, you are the bad guy because you can't help them out even though you have done it plenty of times. That's when the animosity starts to build. They speak badly about you to others in your circle and even to those who are not in your circle. They never bring up all the good things, like how you have been there for them emotionally, physically and financially.

Deep down they may be envious of you or what you have. Their only way to make you look bad is to disclose your secrets to others. Maybe you confided in them about a health issue or marital problems, and they thought it would be best to blast your secrets to the whole family even though you went to them in confidence.

A close family member decided to let everyone in the family know that I was having problems in my marriage after I confided in her. Once other family members started telling me what was said, I realized that the information could have only come from her, because she was the only person in the family who knew. Once I confronted her about it, she acted like she didn't know that she did anything wrong. I even pointed out to her, that when I am speaking with her, it was not for entertainment.

My marriage was in trouble, and I just needed someone to listen to me. Not tell the whole family. Her pattern of spreading your business wasn't isolated to me, as she did this to other family members as well. I should have known better, but I just needed an ear, and she was available. I stopped speaking with her, because she just kept doing the same thing, even after we had conversations about it.

What shortly becomes obvious is that you can no longer trust or confide in that person about your life. Been there and done that. You must remove yourself, because their behavior isn't changing. Unfortunately, if you choose to forgive them and give them another opportunity, they continue to do the same thing. Therefore, while you MUST forgive them you have to remove yourself from the relationship.

Let's face it, some people are miserable and the only way they seem to be happy is when they are disrupting other people lives. Even though you love them, you can't do life with them. They always have a bone to carry, as my grandmother would say. Always in everybody's business, and they don't mind spreading the business even if it's not true. They need and want the attention that it brings to them. To make matters worse, some individuals will go on a tour trying to get others to dislike you, even though you have never done anything to them.

Most mature adults silently move forward once a relationship ends. Others might choose to take a world tour slandering your name because you disagree with or are no longer friends. Suddenly, people that they didn't care for, are now their close friend. Weren't you just speaking negatively about them, but now you are the best of friends. To make matters worse, it is obvious to your circle of friends, that this newfound friend or your interest in them, is not coming from a place of sincerity. You are coming off as fake and disingenuous. Your mutual friends are suddenly taking sides based on what your family member or former friend has said. No one has taken the opportunity to ask your side. They may not realize that the person is trying to slander you and is using them in their game. People you've never interacted with are now making you an enemy. It's hard being around a person you previously had a positive relationship with who suddenly changes their energy.

You can tell when the relationship has changed. But disliking someone because of another's person experience is not Christian-like and there are always three sides to a story. When this happened to me, once my relationship ended with my former best friend, it caught me off guard. But it also confirmed that those individuals really weren't my friends in the first place, if they were, they wouldn't be so willing to only listen to one person's perceptions.

The betrayal is hard to accept when it is a family member betrays you. And other family members expect you to accept the betrayal because they are family. That is totally unrealistic and not healthy. When someone repeatedly disrespects you and you've shared your concerns with them, they don't intend to change. It's up to you to remove yourself from this person. You can't allow others to make you feel guilty about your decision. Encouraging a person to stay in these draining relationships is not healthy and causes greater harm.

Of course, you miss them as a person, but their behavior is just toxic, and you must let it go. How many people have you seen that stay in abusive relationships because they are told to keep forgiving and just tough it out? They will change, they say. But just know, it is okay to put your mental health first and release what is causing the stress and dysfunction.

These kinds of family dysfunctions can be caused by a variety of issues, but greed and sibling rivalry are two main reasons.

Family property and assets, especially when a family member dies, can cause people to argue and fight. Who gets the property? Who gets a family heirloom have resulted in long-time family rifts. And if the family member did not have a will, it can complicate matters. In some instances, parents might designate one person in charge. Generally, it's the one they consider the most responsible. But there are other instances where family members try to swindle each other or fail to follow through with the desires of the deceased.

Some have argued that if property was only left in their name why should they equally distribute it? That is where morals and ethics come into play. Many families have suffered as some members feel betrayed and therefore, distance themselves from their sibling or other family members. In their eyes, something was stolen from them.

I remember an episode of a popular court show where there was a case involving the dispute of funeral and burial costs between two sisters. The plaintiff argued that her mother had a life insurance policy that was for her burial expenses, and upon her death the sisters agreed to use the policy for those expenses. The policy, about $10,000, equaled funeral expenses. The policy was given to the funeral director who realized the policy's beneficiary was in one sister's name. Once she realized this, she cashed the policy, but didn't contribute any of it to her mother's funeral. As a result, the plaintiff personally paid for the funeral.

I couldn't imagine a child not wanting to use the policy as her mother expected. If she was the favorite child, why would she not want her mother to have a proper burial and more importantly why did she feel that she was not responsible to help? But it all came down to greed. When money is involved the urge to do the right thing goes out the window.

This could have been resolved with a will or if people would stop thinking about themselves. While we are living, we have to make sure our last wishes are in writing to eliminate potential family drama.

Sibling rivalry is common. Some children, even when they are adults, are constantly fighting for their parent's attention. Think about Cain and Abel in the Bible, where Cain revolted and killed his brother Abel because of jealousy. What happens when parents prefer one child over another child? For whatever reason, one parent makes it obvious they favor one child over the others. Of course, the less-favored child feels the difference in treatment.

There are no reasons parents should prefer one over the others. Whether it's gender, birth order, physical beauty or whatever, this kind of behavior is common in some families. But this behavior can contribute to sibling rivalry, and this rivalry can lead to more complicated behaviors and broken relationships.

Chapter 8: Friendship Betrayal

Maybe you had a friend who betrayed your trust. They may have dated or married a former boyfriend/girlfriend, shared your business or even stolen from you. Friends, many who can span from childhood to adulthood, are often closer than family members because you have shared experiences with them. They really are our brothers and sisters. When an act of betrayal happens with one of them, it hurts even more than if a stranger had done the same thing.

I have always taken the girl code seriously. I never date a guy that my friend has dated. But now it is a survival-of-the-fittest mentality and people do what is best for them. People are focused on doing what makes them happy despite the circumstances. I have witnessed situations where close friends, male and female, date and even marry their friends' exes. Some might argue well we really weren't friends we just hung out from time to time and supported each other's life events. Whatever they call it now, the reality is you were friends.

None of that matters to some people because their logic is if this individual shows interest in me, and I'm interested in them, they will pursue the relationship. And besides, we are grown, and grown people can do whatever they want to do. I mean, I guess you are right that adults can do whatever they want to do but it is the principle that matters to me. If you have formed a friendship that has lasted decades and even developed bonds with their family, why would you cross that line? Imagine your sibling dating your ex-boyfriend or ex-girlfriend or even your ex-spouse? Some may even argue that if they are not married than it is fair game.

Yes, taking a boy or girlfriend from a friend is bad enough, but stealing from a friend can be worse. They may take something of value from you, or it could be that you loaned them money with the premise that they would pay you back.

We've probably all been that friend that allowed others to borrow money and never got it back. I've had friends and family steal from me. People work hard for their possessions and to have someone to just come take it is a slap in the face. It makes me leery to be around them, if I can't trust them.

I have always heard people say before borrowing money from a friend decide which one you need more – them or the money. That's a lot to think about especially when you have a close friend who needs money to take care of themselves or their family. But while they might need the money, paying it back is another issue. If they didn't have the money in the first place, are they capable of paying it back? I often look at Judge Mathis on TV and a running joke on his show is that you fell for the I will pay you back when I get my income tax line. The reality of it is did you really think you were going to get the money back. For most of us the answer is yes because that individual has a job and surely, they are going to make paying you back a priority even if it's a little bit at a time.

It's sad, but close friends will often leave you in a financial burden. Therefore, it is important not to let people borrow money that is going to put you in a financial bind. It hurts to see them go on vacations and showcase everything they are doing on social media while they still owe you money. When you attempt to setup a repayment arrangement, they avoid your phone calls and even pretend like they are not at home when you pop up. Now, you are more upset not that they owe you money but the fact they are going out of their way to avoid you. As a friend you chose to help them out and they chose to take your kindness as a weakness. Image someone asking to borrow money to avoid being evicted from their home and when you comply you see later on their social media sites that they went to Las Vegas for a concert.

Some people, depending on the amount of money owed, may file a civil lawsuit to get what's owed to them. The fact is, a failure or in some cases refusal to repay what's owed or borrowed, causes relationships to end. Some may survive, but the relationship won't be the same.

Another way friends and family hurt each other is by spreading rumors, intimate information or lies. We are left speechless when we find out that the ones we hold close are often the ones who betray us with rumors. Whether it true or not, it is something you didn't want shared to the public. As a result, it has put you in a negative light. And most often, jealousy is what motivated their actions. They may not like that you advanced in your career before they did, or that you are involved in a relationship, and they are not, or they simply feel that you are beneath them.

When people start acting strange around you or suddenly become unavailable that may be a sign that you need to move past the relationship. No ill will or harm but maybe you have outgrown that person, or you simply don't have the same goals or aspirations. When the relationship ends for whatever reason, you mourn the loss of the friendship. You go through the stages of grief which include denial, anger, bargaining, depression and acceptance. Let's look at the five stages in more detail:

- Denial- We don't want to come to terms with the fact that the individual we once shared life with is no longer in our lives.

- Anger-We get angry when we reflect on the friendship and how easy it was for that person to end it or walk away.

- Bargaining-We tell ourselves things would have been different if we would have kept our opinions to ourselves or if we had supported them more.

- Depression-This feeling of loneliness comes as you are no longer participating in activities with the person or in contact with them.

- Acceptance- Even though we would prefer things to be different, we accept that the friendship is over and move forward.

Ending any relationship can be tough, but we all know that things happen. We must determine how we will let it affect us and how we will move forward. These are two very important factors, as sometimes we get stuck when we are unable to move past situations or people. The loss of my first best friend was hard because I felt that, despite attempts to rekindle the friendship, due to her diagnosis, death took that opportunity away. However, it was easier to deal with, because I felt that in the end, I made myself available for reconciliation.

The loss of my second-best friend was the hardest because I felt that I was discarded after I no longer served a purpose. Not that I had done anything wrong or caused harm, but because I was the single friend. I exhibited all these stages of grief during the loss of this friendship, and from time to time, I still get triggered because I am reminded of activities that we used to do together.

We cannot beat ourselves up when things take a natural course of events. I truly believe that God or your higher being will replace what you have lost and increase it as well. Especially when there was no ill intent or actions on your behalf. My circle of friends remains strong, and those individuals continue to make me a priority in their lives. I am respectful that our time together may be limited to life events, but we are still committed to making the relationship work.

Chapter 9: Church Trauma

For most people, their place of worship is where they go to bond with others and develop a relationship with a higher power. It is a place of renewal, safety and refuge. Not that it is exempt from issues, but it is also the place where people think they will be free from hurt, harm or danger. For me, church is a place of renewal and a judgment-free zone. Growing up, my family didn't attend church. My grandma would listen to the service on the radio on Sunday morning, but during my childhood, she did not physically attend. She did, however, make sure that I attended.

I attended a Holiness church, and I was lucky enough that church members would come pick me up. Every Sunday, my grandma made sure I was ready, and either the church's first lady or one of her children picked me up. I don't recall having a negative church experience.

Growing up Holiness was like a full-time job. Sunday School would start at 10 a.m., followed by morning worship. It may be around 2-3 p.m. before church adjourns for the day. Since I didn't have a family member at the church, the church elders made sure to correct me if I fell asleep during service. We had the same pastor the entire time I was there, and it stayed that way until I attended college. These experiences laid the foundation for my faith, and while I was young, the scripture and my church family reminded me that God was faithful and that if we lean on him for all understanding and our needs, he will provide. It wasn't until my adulthood that I realized that sometimes church folk, not the church, will condemn you to hell.

In college, we had chapel service every Tuesday on campus, and while there was usually a good word, I was just used to a different style of service. While there, I also attended a church of a similar denomination, not too far from campus. One of my classmates and I would frequent the church from time to time. Overall, I enjoyed the service and fellowship. But that all changed. I noticed a young lady, dressed in white and with a head slip on, sitting in the back of the church.

She didn't look to be any more than maybe 14 or 15 years old, and she was pregnant. I was wondering, why was she sitting there isolated from everybody else? I'm pretty sure her parents attended the same church. I asked one of the members why she was sitting by herself when there was more than enough room for her to sit closer or with someone. The response I received disappointed me. The church member said that because she was an unwed mother that she had to sit in the back.

What kind of foolishness was that? This young lady made a mistake, and I add, not by herself, and she is being shamed and told to sit in the back of the church? Not trying to justify anything, but I am pretty sure if God had taken an inventory of sins committed, no one in that church could come forward with clean hands. It was probably already a traumatic experience being pregnant at such a young age, and I am pretty sure, based on her isolation in church, her family probably wasn't supportive. I can only guess since she was sitting there alone.

I know life doesn't go as planned, and we should be honest with the facts, but do we continue to crucify the individual for the sin? It is up to her to go to the Lord and ask forgiveness. The church had no reason to judge her.

But church folk, to the surprise of some, can cause a great deal of pain. I know that my Savior has always been there for me, and therefore I will remain faithful to him. When acts of betrayal happen at church, it can lead to individuals withdrawing from their faith, instead of withdrawing from the people. Therefore, when an act of betrayal happens at the church, the trauma from this experience can cause a person to lose faith in others and trust and faith in their higher power.

Historically, the African American community sought the refuge of the church to help heal and bring solace to their community. During slavery, Jim Crow and even today's church, our place of worship is where we go to lay all our burdens down. It is supposed to be a place of no judgment and where genuine relationships happen.

However, some church folks are often the reason for confusion and chaos. It is often a place of competition as individuals are competing for a spot in the choir, competing to be over the women's auxiliary board or competing for the pastor's attention.

I attempted to participate as a choir member once, and let's just say after hearing myself sing a couple of times, I realized it wasn't my ministry, and I graciously stepped down. Of course, we should go to church to form a closer relationship with God, but we do know that people also come to be entertained. It's like the church is a business. Individuals look at it for several reasons including what religion is being practiced, what auxiliaries are offered, what is the church's size or what is the male-to-female ratio? What is the age range of the congregation? What time and day of the week is the service and so forth.

Once they have found their church home, they are ready to get involved and form new relationships. For many auxiliary leaders, the church or church leadership requires that members have experience and some formal educational background. But for many people, they just want to serve and have a passion for whatever group or organization they choose to volunteer for.

They aren't trying to be perfect; they just want to do the best job they can for the God they serve. But and this is where the issues start, some church leadership is looking for perfection or select people, leaving others left out.

I remember looking at an episode of "Mama's Family," where Mama Harper was trying to get in the good graces of Pastor and First Lady Meechum, so she would be over the church's women's auxiliary group. To do this, she figured that she would invite them over for Sunday dinner and allow them to fellowship with her and her family and this would give her an opportunity to toot her own horn and speak about her work in the church. Inviting the pastor and their family over for Sunday dinner is quite normal in the South, and believe it or not, there is competition to see who gets to feed the pastor. Mama Harper made sure the house was in order, and nothing was out of place. She gave everyone a lecture about making sure things were clean and that everyone was on their best behavior.

I can imagine something similar happens if the pastor plans to visit your home. The point here is that the pastor is looked up to as the head of the church; therefore, individuals often go out of their way to make sure they are pleasing or impressing the pastor. While this behavior is appropriate, we must also remember why we are attending church – a closer relationship with God, not the pastor.

Often, when some members aren't selected to serve where they want, they take the denial personally. And this church hurt can be the worse because they felt this was one place where they would be immune to such. Now don't get me wrong if you truly aren't qualified for the position, you shouldn't just be in the position.

Church hurt leaves people questioning God rather than the church people. What we often fail to understand is that everything that happens in church isn't godly. We have people who are professional church attendees, wouldn't dare miss a service or program, but they don't have God in them. Their words do not match their actions. Even for some pastors, Sunday service is a performance. It sounds good and looks good, but there are no opportunities for people to build relationships with God. When you leave church, you realize that the leader's actions are not lining up with their sermons. God sees everything, and if individuals are not doing the right thing it will eventually catch up with them.

Let me be clear, my words aren't an indictment of all clergy or all church members. But to ignore that church is a place where people can and do get hurt would be shortsighted.

We should evaluate our relationship with our God and determine what we want out of the relationship. We also have to acknowledge that humans are subject to error, and we shouldn't be surprised when they make mistakes. Even while we are in the church. We cannot allow these mistakes to hinder us from becoming closer to our God. No church is perfect, but we must really evaluate if that church body can feed us spiritually and if we are willing to form a closer relationship with God on our own.

We should also spend time with God outside of church. We can read and study the Bible, meditate, pray and participate in those activities that help make our community stronger and lift the status of people in our community. Church fellowship and support is great, but it's not the only places where we can meet God. Get to know God and His word for yourself. Then, maybe whatever you might have thought happened can be overlooked or maybe it's time to find another place of worship. Just don't let church people and their hurt stop you from having a relationship with God.

Chapter 10: Act of Forgiving

We've spent a lot of time looking at the different types of trauma and broken relationships, but the key message here is that we must decide for ourselves how to move forward. You may never receive an apology or acknowledgment from an individual(s) that you feel has harmed or betrayed you. But you can't stop living and thriving. How you move forward will determine your happiness or are you going to let trauma control your life. Don't give anybody or any situation that kind of power.

Webster's dictionary defines forgive as "cease to feel resentment against or to give up resentment of or claim to requital." Forgiving your abuser, family or former friend means relinquishing the feelings of resentment. It does not, however, mean that the memory of their act disappears, but that you have chosen to forgive them for the act. We might wonder, "How could I forgive someone who has done such horrible things to me?". The truth is, we must forgive because God forgave us for our sins. As Christians, forgiveness allows us to move toward healing and growth.

The Bible references several scriptures that address forgiveness. Let's take a further look at them. Ephesians 4:32 says, "be kind and compassionate to one another, forgiving each other, just as in Christ God forgave you." Matthew 18:21-22 says, "Then Peter came to Jesus and asked, "Lord how many times shall I forgive my brother or sister who sins against me?' Up to seven times? Jesus answered, "I tell you, not seven times, but seventy-seven times."

Really. Seventy-seven is a high number, but as Christians, we should forgive no matter how many times a person wrongs us. Of course, at some point, we must evaluate who are we surrounding ourselves with or why are we putting ourselves in positions where we must constantly forgive someone. Are we making good decisions? A prime example would be allowing yourself to continuously go back to a relationship where you are being disrespected repeatedly. While we cannot control others' actions, we can be mindful of how people treat us. If someone disrespects, you through any form of abuse or simply refuses to respect your boundaries and they do this repeatedly at some point you have to limit your interaction with them or walk away. Relationships are hard, but there must be an evaluation of the relationship if it's causing harm.

The truth is, because we care and love someone, it is hard to walk away. We must give it to God and ask him to remove those who do not have our best interests at heart. You must be prepared for what they may look like, because when he starts working, your circle may become a little smaller.

I've seen firsthand where fellow Christians have encouraged their family and friends to stay in an abusive or toxic relationship because God forgives. First Corinthians 15:33, says, "bad company corrupts good character," and in Proverbs 22:24-25 it says, "do not make friends with a hot-tempered person, do not associate with one easily angered or you may learn their ways and get yourself ensnared." The Bible tells us that it is okay to let go of relationships that hinder your development and growth, and more importantly, that interfere with your relationship with God.

I've heard so many Christians say I forgave my spouse for cheating regularly because I believe in my vows. Individuals do change and can stop the cheating and lying, but often they just continue. They continue to see other individuals throughout the marriage, and they are so comfortable cheating that they go out on dates with them, have children outside the marriage and even take vacations with them. There is no behavior change and if we want to really look at the Bible, one of the commandments says, "thou should not commit adultery." Therefore, the same people encouraging you to forgive should also be looking at the same Bible they are quoting. At some point, their decision to stay is because that's what they want.

Matthew 5:15 says, "but if you do not forgive others their sins, your Father will not forgive your sins." Some might argue this is not fair as someone has deliberately done something to harm you, but it doesn't matter, you still have to forgive them. It's like we are asking God to do something for us that we can't do for others.

If we explore this even further, we not only need to forgive others, we need to forgive ourselves. While some events in your life are of no fault of your own or maybe it was the results of a bad decision(s).

We sometimes want to play the victim card when certain events don't turn out in our favor, but the reality is that there will be negative repercussions for negative actions. If you make the conscious decision to do something that you know is morally and legally wrong, you'd better believe there is going to be a consequence to it.

Personally, there were probably a couple of my relationships that were red flags from the beginning. But because those individuals treated me well, or at least that's what I thought, I continued to stay with them. In the end, it got me nowhere. Not only was it time to go, but I left hurt. When I went back and did some soul searching, I should never have even gotten involved. Lessons were learned, and I moved on. I took responsibility for the role I played in the situation, however I asked for forgiveness and moved forward. I had to ask myself to evaluate my patterns and why was I choosing to involve myself with individuals who were not emotionally available and physically available to me. I had to make better choices and live with the consequences of the bad choices previously made.

No longer was I going to allow my past mistakes to keep me hostage. I made mistakes, and even though I made mistakes, I still deserved to be happy. I acknowledge the part I had to play in my own setbacks and heartaches, but I can't hold on to those things. I asked God to forgive me and to give me strength to move forward. I had to tell myself that if I continued to dwell on the past, I was putting my future in a hostage state.

If you make a mistake and God gives you an opportunity to live to see another day, then you have the chance to correct your mistakes and move past them. I think the song by gospel artist Donnie McClurkin, says it all, "We fall down, but we get up. For a saint is just a sinner who falls down." Those lyrics remain a constant reminder to me, that I will make mistakes, but I will have an opportunity to learn from those mistakes and look forward to another day. Each day I am given an opportunity to live, I make a conscious effort to focus on the things I do have control over.

Forgiving ourselves is critical. Questioning a mistake that we made in our 20s should not mean that you blame yourself for the next 20 years. You did something wrong; there were consequences. Hopefully you learned from them, and now it is time to move on. Once you ask God for forgiveness, he forgives you! Therefore, forgive yourself and learn from the experience.

I choose to forgive myself for past mistakes that God has already forgiven me for. One thing about God, if he provides one opportunity, he will provide another. We must, however, make sure when another opportunity presents itself, we take it. There is never a time that we can't achieve our dreams.

I'm almost 50 years old, and I am still going after things that are on my bucket list. I look at it like this, my daughter is an adult, and I now have the free time to commit to achieving some of my goals. The truth is that people start over every day, and with hard work and determination, they can fulfill their dreams and aspirations. So, you're older now. Now you have more experience, wisdom and patience and can objectively and logically work toward accomplishing your dreams and desires.

In addition to forgiving ourselves, we must move beyond wanting to retaliate against those who hurt us. It's only human nature that you want to do something to get back at them. Someone has hurt you, and you want them to feel the pain they inflicted upon you. However, the Bible say that vengeance belongs to God. Romans 12:19 states, "beloved, never avenge yourselves, but leave it to the wrath of God, for it is written, "vengeance is mine, I will repay, says the lord.' I would be kidding myself if I said, I would love to respond to all the subliminal social media posts, however, I will let God fight those battles.

By responding, I only create another negative experience and more ill will. Therefore, I am just going to let it go, for my peace and my accountability. If we take the time to evaluate things, we will see that in some situations God has already worked it out. There was no need for you to get them back, because God did it.

Now, the Bible doesn't give a timeframe of when God is going to inflict vengeance, and this is where we sometimes try to take matters into our hands. Because we don't see it —or because it appears the person who has harmed us is living a carefree life —we think it is time for us to act. We then try to do things to cause harm. But just because we don't physically see things does not mean that that person or persons aren't suffering from their consequences. That person or persons may have suffered tremendous setbacks because of their actions; however, God is a merciful God in that he does not inflict pain forever. Therefore, they can move on and hopefully learn from their mistakes.

We may never see any form of punishment in our lifetime, but that doesn't mean that the person(s) who caused you harm will not receive punishment. The same way God forgives us is the same way he is going to forgive the individual who has caused you pain. No matter how hard this is for us to hear, God will also forgive those who have abused you if they ask for forgiveness. This is really a tough subject for some, but the truth is, God can change anybody. Notice I said God can change anybody, meaning not me, you or family/friend can make anyone change. If we seek the Lord and ask him to change our ways, He will do just that.

Moving past the hurt and pain means taking it day by day. Not to sound like a broken record, but we must make the mental decision that we want to move forward. That is accepting that you can't change what has happened, but you can change how you respond to it. Also, while it is easy to focus on all the negative things, it is also easy to find something to be grateful for.

This can be done through journaling and reciting positive affirmations. Start your day off with thankfulness and give praise to God or your higher being for waking you up in the morning, for being able to speak, thankfulness for being able to move your body, thankfulness for the home you are able to wake up in, thankfulness for the food you eat, the job that pays your bills, the health insurance to pay your medical bills and the healthy body that you have. If you really focus, I am pretty sure that you can find at least five things to be thankful for.

Releasing what has happened to you or your experience, means releasing it verbally. Have you ever felt relief by just talking to someone about your situation? When your body releases stress, the brain releases and reduces stress hormones, including adrenaline and cortisol, which helps to relax your muscles, drop your blood pressure and heart rate. If you are keeping your emotions and feelings suppressed, it leads to anxiety, depression, headaches, fatigue, sleeplessness, high blood pressure and other issues. To get beyond the hurt, you must accept the things that you cannot change.

Are you ready to move forward and if so, what steps are you willing to take to do so? It starts with this simple question, and the hardest part is making the decision to move forward. For me, I acknowledged that I needed to do something different. I stay in constant prayer, particularly for God to control my emotions and to remove all hurt, harm and danger from my life. I have several notebooks that I journal my thoughts in, and this helps me to release stress and express how I feel. I pay attention to my emotions, and when I sense that I am not my normal self, I follow up with my counselor for a session(s).

Before, when I would get invitations to attend activities, I would just say "yes" because I was happy to be considered. However, "no" is now in my vocabulary because overextending myself is just adding to my stress. My friends laugh at me, because on the weekends I take a nap between 4 and 5 p.m. I am so busy with work, church and sorority activities during the week, I often don't get to bed until after 11p.m., and it takes a while for me to winddown. Therefore, when the opportunity presents itself, I take a nap. I can't operate on fumes, and eventually my body will slow down.

These are just a couple things I do to reset, but I am aware they are all necessary for me to recharge and to work toward my growth and healing.

Chapter 11: Let Go And Let God

In my 48 years of life, I have experienced heartache, pain and disappointment. While I can say that some of my pain was caused by others, I also acknowledge that I caused some of my pain and disappointment as well. There is nothing I can do about the past; however, I can reflect on the choices I made and what led me to involve myself in situations that may not have had my best interest at heart. Those individuals who simply did not do the right thing by me, may never acknowledge the pain they have caused me; however, I have made the decision to forgive them anyway.

One of the first things I reflected on was there was something wrong, and that I needed outside counsel. While I consider myself a Southern Baptist Christian, I also realize that we have mental health counselors for a reason.

I have prayed about forgiveness and healing; however, I realized that I needed to verbalize how I was feeling in a neutral setting to an individual who was unaware of me or my situation and not be judged. Let's face it, everyone can't relate to what you may be going through because they have never experienced it. Therefore, it is important to talk to someone to make sure you are providing self-care.

I support speaking to your pastor, but if we evaluate the educational background of our spiritual leaders, many are not trained to deal with the trauma of sexual, physical or mental abuse. Of course, they can offer guidance regarding forgiveness, however, in some situations, only medical treatment can resolve the issue.

It was through person-centered counseling that I realized I could be disappointed in my choices and the choices of others, but I had the power to move past my situation(s) and heal from my experiences. For me, that looked like having accountability for my actions, having empathy for those who hurt me and having self-awareness of settings and people who may trigger any past hurt.

There is nothing I can do to change the actions of others, but I can express how I feel if someone is hurting me. People often tell you to suck it up, you will get over it or they are unaware that their actions affected you. I believe it is important to express how you feel or remove yourself from an uncomfortable situation when your concern falls on deaf ears.

To be empathetic or have empathy means the act of understanding, being aware of, being sensitive to and vicariously experiencing the feelings, thoughts and experiences of another. Can we really have empathy for someone who has caused us pain? A way to look at this is that normally, people are repeating a cycle of abuse that has been inflicted on them, and because it was left untreated, the individual(s) continued the pattern of misbehavior.

We can have empathy for them because they have also suffered, but because nothing was done to help them, they are now causing pain to others. When individuals bring up your past to keep you in the past, consider maybe they are having life regrets about their choices, and the only way they can feel better about themselves is to bring up your past.

I know, it makes sense but doesn't make sense. Imagine if you are given all the opportunities including finances, education, resources and family support; however, you, for whatever reason, didn't take advantage of those opportunities and a family member or friend who has maybe had less opportunities or some legal trouble fulfills their legal obligation but then can recover from the negative situation and build their own successful business. I mean, one would think the person who hasn't had any legal trouble would be more advanced in their career; however, if you don't have the drive or motivation to do anything differently, your situation doesn't change. If we look at this situation, we could understand how they may feel, but once again, it doesn't mean they have to keep bringing up your past to make themselves feel better.

Once I realized that the behavior of others was not going to change, even when I expressed how I felt, I knew that I could no longer entertain those individuals or put myself in settings where I had to be around them. For some, this could be difficult because those places are usually family gatherings.

While you may not have an issue with everyone who is in the same place as you, it may be in your best interest to avoid them or limit your time there. One thing about family and people in general is that they can be aware of the issue or what has happened, but they expect you to keep putting up with the disrespect just because you are family.

Once again, this is unacceptable. Those same individuals should consider why the person(s) continues to behave this way. On another note, just because we forgive them for their actions does not mean that we must reconcile the relationship. This is so important to understand. Trying to reconcile a relationship or build one that never existed when there is unchanged behavior is a recipe for disaster. While some relationships can be saved because of repentance and changed behavior, others cannot because the opposite has not occurred. Also, if we are being realistic, no one wants to have a relationship with the person(s) who abused them.

Forgiving yourself and others is the only way to move past your trauma. An apology or acknowledgment may never be received, but we, as Christians, must rely on God to avenge those who have wronged us and move forward. Resentment only leads to anger, and if we are full of anger and resentment, we prevent ourselves from being happy and enjoying life. Life happens and life is what you make it as they say, and we cannot do anything about the action of others, but we can control how we respond to their actions.

I believe in God and therapy, and I know individuals may not be comfortable going to a stranger and talking about their issues. However, it is often necessary when we are trying to heal, move forward and regroup. No one wants to be the bag lady or bag man and carry trauma and unresolved issues into our relationships. The consequences are never good, and individuals just continue hurting others because hurt people hurt people. We need God and counseling to get through this thing called life.

One of my favorite songs is" Let's go crazy" by one of the greatest entertainers of all time, Prince. I never really paid attention to the lyrics, but when you really take the time to evaluate them, this song is the reality of what we should be doing. He speaks about the afterworld, but he also emphasizes that we are all going to die. I know no one wants to think about that, but God said there would be life and death. I think the lyrics below sum up what we should be doing.

We're all excited (all excited)

Don't know why (I don't know why).

Maybe it's' cause

We're all gonna die.

What's it all for? (What's it all for?)

Better live now

Before the grim reaper comes knocking on your door.

Tell me, are we gonna let the elevator bring us down?

Oh no, let's go

Let's go crazy (let's go crazy).

Let's get nuts (let's get nuts).

Let's look for the purple banana

Until they put us back in the truck, let's go.

The phrase, "better live now," stands out the most to me. We must determine whether we will let our past or circumstances hinder us from living our lives. I am pretty sure if we take the time to sit down and talk with our peers, friends and family, at least one person can tell you about a traumatic event that has happened to them. To take things even further, those same people can also tell you how they were able to move forward.

We must be intentional about our choices, especially the ones we can control. We must change our surroundings, broaden our horizons, be open to change and make the conscious decision to live better. If we constantly have the" woe is me attitude, then we are just setting ourselves up for negative things to continue in our lives. Even more so, who wants to be around negative people all the time? It ruins your mood, and, in some cases, it may even trigger you. Let's face it, life has not always been great for some of us, however, we are the masters of our fate, and we must make the decision how we are going to live our lives.

Chapter 12: Letting Go

Learning to Let Go: When the apology is not there, it's really everyone's story. We must heal from our past, seek professional help if needed and more importantly, we must let God guide our lives. There is no such thing as perfect, but we can strive to have a better quality of life for ourselves and, more importantly, for those we love. The reality is that people who you feel have wronged you may never own up to it, and some might even blame you for their actions. It is unfortunate, but we must realize that we cannot change people, and some people are fighting their own demons. We cannot let their actions sabotage our opportunity for healing and growth. Trauma, when left untreated, often leads to repeated cycles of abuse, unhealthy relationships and lack of trust. It is normal to surround yourself with individuals who acknowledge your feelings, support your needs, respect you and, more importantly, who you can share life with.

Instead of making New Year's resolutions, strive to improve your life throughout the year. Whether that is through prayer and fasting, journaling, seeking pastoral care or going to counseling. Work through your triggers and identify what you need to do to move past them. That does not mean you still will not have them, but you talk about what happened. I know this is very painful, but I promise you will feel a sense of release once you acknowledge what has happened and how it has made you feel. From there, you can focus on healing, whether you receive acknowledgement or an apology from them.

We cannot focus on what is important in life if we are unwilling to address issues affecting us and our loved ones. Forgiveness is about being able to move forward and live your authentic life. Your traumatic experience can cause you to carry a heavy load of pain, guilt and anger. Built-up anger leads to so many things, and most of it leads to unhealthy relationships or a lack of relationships because we choose not to address our trauma.

For some, isolation is a part of their daily routine because they have not faced what has happened to them, and they are unwilling to confront their situation. It's too painful to even think about, let alone, be around or enter the place that caused the pain. No one knows the time it takes for the pain to go away or when it gets easier to deal with, but what we do know is that if left untreated, it only leads to other issues. Unresolved trauma can lead to unhealthy relationships or, more importantly, an unwillingness to create new ones.

We owe it to ourselves to make our mental health a top priority to ensure a good quality of life. You owe it to yourself to resolve your trauma and to make healthy decisions regarding your life. More importantly, it causes stress and anxiety which could lead to other things.

If you have never experienced any form of trauma, count yourself lucky. According to the National Counseling for Behavioral Health, 70% of adults in the United States have experienced some type of traumatic event at least once in their lifetime. If we break that number down, that equates to about 223.4 million people. This is a huge number. So, while you may not have experienced trauma, it happens, and there is a need to receive treatment.

Empathy can go a long way when we encounter people who have experienced trauma. Being mindful that your experiences may not look like someone else's is key to avoiding judging people. We can change our circumstances and surroundings; however, we cannot change people. Change must begin with us, and the first step is accepting that something needs realignment. Mental stability often leads to stability in one's life, whether it is financial, emotional or spiritual. I encourage you to take a leap of faith and start your healing process —not only to heal from the past, but also to begin your future.

Chapter 13: Self-Care

Quite often, when the cares of this world take over, we forget to do the little things to improve our physical and emotional well-being. Life goes on, and we simply cannot stop living. If we continue to operate like an electric fan, we will eventually lose our power. We must take care of our mind, body and soul, and make every effort to enjoy life. I am sure if we take a step back, we can find something to be thankful for. We are not free from trials and tribulations; however, we cannot let them consume us.

Self-care is defined as the practice of taking action to preserve or improve one's health. As individuals, experiences that has occurred in childhood or adulthood have impacted our lives. Some of the situations were simply out of your control, and you cannot continue to let them impact your life. You must be aware of your triggers and work to address them. Think about it this way: you cannot go into spaces and expect everyone to cater their interactions to you because you may be triggered.

Now, that doesn't mean that you can't be asked to be respected, but most people have no idea of what you have experienced. Some people are genuinely trying to have a good time and are not aware that the person sharing the same space may be having an episode because of something you may have said or done. This is why it is so important to take the necessary steps to heal and recover.

My mental health matters is not just a statement, but it is a part of my daily living. I consider myself a Christian, flaws and all, and therefore I study the word and seek God through prayer. My pastor always refers me to the scripture, and one scripture that I rely on is, "Philippians 4:13, "I can do all things through Christ who strengthens me." It is a reminder to me that my strength comes from God, and with his support, nothing is impossible. I remind myself of God's promises and the scriptures help. In addition, I also seek counseling as needed. My current employer offers six free visits through the Employee Assistance Program, and I take advantage of it as needed.

For me, being able to just speak freely, without being judged, helps me to release my emotions. My counselor can confirm my feelings, and as a team we can focus on resolving whatever conflict I have. Even though no one is free from sin, sometimes our elders and pastor cannot see beyond the sin, to focus on forgiveness and healing. Being in a judge-free zone, helps with the problem's resolution.

Peace and quiet work for me as well, as I find that sitting and meditating helps to clear my thoughts and focus. Turning my electronic devices off and sitting in silence allows me to really tune into my thoughts. When I identify there are changes in my mood, I limit my interaction with others and reflect on what is really bothering me. Because I don't have a counselor on speed dial, when I realize that my emotions are out of sorts, I will reach out to a close friend to vent.

Through the trials in my life, I have learned that saying "No" is for my self-preservation. Nothing personal, but I cannot overextend myself and expect things to get better. Therefore, I am beginning to say no, and even to suggest getting someone else to do it. I mean, I took pride in always being available to help others, but while we are supposed to help, there are limits. Also, saying no for me preserves relationships. I learned this the hard way with my best friend who passed and through the relationship with my grandmother. In a nutshell, I take things day by day and aim to remain in the present.

Let's look at some of the suggested activities below for self-care. While this list is not exhaustive, anyone can take at least one or two of these suggestions and work toward achieving them. It is important to remember that you must do things at your own pace. You cannot compare your situation to anyone else's. The important thing is that you are making an attempt to incorporate doing these things.

Journaling and reading a daily motivation are easy activities that eventually lead to doing others on this list. Travel can be tricky because we know everything is so expensive; however, a mini vacation can be as simple as traveling an hour away to a nearby city. Visiting your local parks and taking a nature walk is free. Many city tours are inexpensive, and there are always festivals of some sort happening in your local area.

The United States has so many wonderful historic sites, national parks, lakes, flower gardens, canyons, museums, vineyards and much more. Therefore, while it is nice to have your passport, you can still relax right here in the United States or even at home.

I used to be one of those people who would not go out to dinner or a movie by myself. Now, I do it with no problem. Everyone has a busy schedule, and sometimes it's easier and better to go alone to gather your thoughts. Dinner with a friend is always nice, but it's okay to be in your own presence. If we don't take care of our mind and body, eventually they will break down.

Talking to someone in your faith community or a counselor can help release tension and stress. Stress can lead to major health issues such as anxiety, depression, exhaustion, heart issues and other health issues. If we are not good to ourselves, how can we pour into our families and communities? Better yet, how can we pour into ourselves if we are not resting and working through our challenges? There is always something to do, but we must set aside at least 30 minutes to an hour each day to practice self-care.

Letting go when the apology is not there is for the preservation of our own mental health. Have you ever encountered someone who is always negative? They never have anything positive to say, and they always look for the bad. I mean, it could be something as simple as you verbalizing that you want to go see the new movie, and that person will immediately say something like, "Well, I heard it was no good." They aren't willing to see it for themselves and base everything on what they heard or some internet conspiracy. They approach everything the same way.

I can remember a deaconess that attended my former church and every time you would speak and ask her how she was doing, you could never get a positive response. It was always something negative, it could be my back hurts or this hurts. All you could do was smile and advise her that you pray that her health improves and to have a great day. I mean, a deaconess is a leader in the church, if you are always negative what is that saying to others about your faith. It's like they have a spirit of negativity and are always Debbie Downers.

Carrying the baggage around slowly steals our joy and hinders us from becoming what God intends us to be. No one wants to be around those kinds of people.

If we look at Psalms 46:3-5 (New International Version) it says, "I will praise you as long as I live, and in your name, I will lift up my hands," and "God is within her, she will not fall; God will help her at the break of day." We must continue to praise God and lean on him for strength and understanding. He will order our steps, and more importantly, he will heal the wounded, fight our battles and restore our joy. If we can choose anything in life, let us choose to live life more abundantly and without regrets. When I refer to God's word, I am reminded that he has my fate in his hands, therefore, I will continue to praise him. I will praise him through worship and prayer. Spending this time with him takes me to my happy place. Have you ever noticed that once you decide to allow God to handle your problems, it is like a burden is lifted off of you?? The weight is gone, and you can finally begin to see the light at the end of the tunnel. We are the masters of our own fate and conquerors through him who loved us. You may never get that apology but letting go and moving forward is necessary for your healing and growth. Please choose to live life today and not focus on things of yesterday.

Self-Care Ideas to help you Relax, Relate and Release

1. Invest in individual and family counseling (being able to express yourself in a non-judgmental zone is beneficial.)
2. Journal and write down your thoughts. (Release it on paper.)
3. Exercise at least three times a week. (Take a walk in your neighborhood or local park.)
4. Read a daily motivation!
5. Volunteer and help others!
6. Gardening.
7. Take yourself out on a date.
8. Take a mini vacation.
9. Go to a comedy show.
10. Say "no" more often. (There is nothing like being in a place or around people that make you uncomfortable.)
11. Read a book.
12. Sleep (most adults need seven to nine hours of sleep each day).
13. Take a bubble bath and light a candle.
14. Eat healthy meals.
15. Connect with a faith community.
16. Listen to music/go to a concert.
17. Get that deep tissue massage.
18. Make a hair appointment.
19. Get a manicure and pedicure.
20. Go to the museum.

Please consider these mental health resources as you explore healing and growth. As I previously stated, we sometimes need a counselor *and* a preacher.

Resources

EAP (Employee Assistance Program) - Most employers offer support and resources to address personal and work-related challenges and concerns. This service is free, and it usually covers four to six visits annually.

https://www.christiancounselordirectory.com (Free online resource for locating Christian counselors.)

https://www.ncblcmhc.org (Free online resource that allows individuals to search for professional counselors, social workers and mental health professionals in North Carolina.)

https://www.nbcc.org (Free online resource that allows individuals to search for nationally certified professional counselors and mental health professionals.)

https://www.psychologytoday.com (Free online resource that allows individuals to search for professional counselors, social workers and mental health professionals in their area.)

National Sexual Assault Hotline **800-656-4673.**

National Suicide - Hotline - 988lifeline.org, 988 phone number.

Today I choose to forgive because?

_____
_____
_____
_____
_____
_____
_____
_____
_____
_____
_____
_____
_____
_____
_____
_____
_____
_____
_____
_____
_____
_____
_____
_____
_____
_____
_____
_____
_____
_____
_____
_____

Today I choose to forgive myself because?

_____
_____
_____
_____
_____
_____
_____
_____
_____
_____
_____
_____
_____
_____
_____
_____
_____
_____
_____
_____
_____
_____
_____
_____
_____
_____
_____
_____
_____
_____

What are three things I can immediately do to start my self-care routine, and what is my plan?

Action:

_____
_____
_____
_____
_____
_____

Plan:

_____
_____
_____
_____
_____

Action:

_____
_____
_____
_____
_____
_____

Plan:

_____
_____
_____
_____
_____
_____

Action:

_____
_____
_____
_____
_____
_____

Plan:

_____
_____
_____
_____
_____

Action:

_____
_____
_____
_____
_____
_____

Plan:

_____
_____
_____
_____
_____

Action:

_____
_____
_____
_____
_____
_____
_____

Plan:

_____
_____
_____
_____
_____

Action:

_____
_____
_____
_____
_____
_____
_____

Plan:

_____
_____
_____
_____
_____
_____

Results cannot be provided if there is no
"Changed Behavior"

www.ingramcontent.com/pod-product-compliance
Lightning Source LLC
Chambersburg PA
CBHW060642130626
46555CB00002B/913